MANAGING STRESS IN MINISTRY

Managing Stress
in Ministry

WILLIAM E. HULME

Harper & Row, Publishers, San Francisco

Cambridge, Hagerstown, New York, Philadelphia
London, Mexico City, São Paulo, Singapore, Sydney

FIRST EDITION

Designer: Jim Mennick

Library of Congress Cataloging in Publication Data

Hulme, William Edward.
  MANAGING STRESS IN MINISTRY.

  Bibliography: p.
  Includes index.
  1. Clergy—Psychology.   2. Clergy—Religious life.
3. Stress (Psychology)   I. Title.
BV4398.H84   1985   253'.2   84-48221
ISBN 0-06-064077-4

---

85 86 87 88 89 10 9 8 7 6 5 4 3 2 1

Contents

7/391

Preface

The pressures peculiar to the parish ministry have long been a concern of mine. While challenged in a most positive way by this vocation, I also experienced its tensions. I was made most aware of this when I left the parish ministry for a college chaplaincy. I found myself with unfilled time in the evening! It was a new experience.

In the following years, my specialization in pastoral counseling has kept me in close touch with the parish ministry. Through clergy conferences, retreats, workshops, and requests for clergy counseling, I have become even more aware of the pressures of this wonderful but impossible calling. Just recently a lay leader shared with me the sad story of his pastor's resignation. "He tried so hard to keep on top of things," he said, "but it was obviously too much. His health has given out. Now instead of doing everything well, he is unable to do anything." So often is this the dilemma of a perfectionist in a perfection-defying profession.

Yet these pressures are not solely the pastor's problem. The congregation also has a responsibility for the pastor's welfare. Because it seemed to me that many congregations did not recognize their involvement in clergy stress, I directed my first attempt to confront this problem to the laity and entitled it *Your Pastor's Problems* (1966).

Since then much has been written on the phenomenon of stress, specifically *dis*tress, with much emphasis on its harmful effect on one's body, mind, spirit, relationships, work, and personal satisfaction. This information has been particularly relevant to the parish ministry because of its high stress character. There also has been much written on ways to ameliorate stress, obviously also applicable to the parish minister. Yet clergy have distinct resources for this amelioration in their own religious tradition. In fact, the ministry itself is a ministry in the stresses of life and is by its very nature a stress reducer. The resource for this stress reduction is the pastor's own religious tradition of reconciliation and peace. I do not believe that this particular potential of the tradition has been sufficiently recognized, so in this book I have tried not only to recognize it but to assist clergy in the actualization of it for their own welfare.

This tradition is basically a theology of grace—of unconditional love, of forgiveness, of power for change. Our challenge as clergy is to let this theology inform our own inner life, shape our own motivations, speak to our own concerns, and influence our own emotions.

I introduce the subject in Chapter 1 by raising the question of why parish clergy may be stressed and finding the answer in the built-in stressors of the vocation. Chapter 2 is a survey of the current research data regarding the harmful effects of stress on the body, mind, and spirit. In Chapter 3, I examine our cultural values and priorities as sources for stress for clergy as well as laypersons. The association of stress with one's job is the focus of Chapter 4, including the way in which the clergy job reflects the job mentality of our culture.

Chapter 5 begins the focus on the religious resources for coping with this stress, specifically the influence of one's religious faith on how one interprets any present moment. Chapter 6 deals with the practice of prayer as a dialogical resource for the support of this perspective of faith. Chapter 7 takes up the role of life-style in stress and the need for balancing the life-style to reduce stress. I discuss the dynamic of trust in Chapter 8, especially its role in enabling us to take control of our own lives, and emotions. Chapter 9 deals with interpersonal relationships, especially the strained relationships with the congregation and the family that create stress—and with the biblical resources for interpersonal dialogue.

Because of the many demands on their attention, clergy can easily procrastinate in making difficult decisions until they are made for them. Chapter 10 explores ways clergy can make these decisions themselves as a way of reducing stress. Chapter 11 focuses on the need to replace distress with good stress (eustress) and on the utilization of religious resources such as serenity and enthusiasm to stimulate such stresses. Chapter 12 places the stress-reducing resources of our religious tradition within the perspective of the crucifixion and resurrection of Christ, specifically using the theology of the cross and the theology of resurrection and victory to illustrate both the realism and the hope needed for living in a fallen world. The epilogue is a concluding statement on the wisdom of integrating the data of science on stress with a theological base for religious help in order to provide a more holistic approach to this very human problem.

Among those to whom I am particularly indebted for my own learning in the management of stress in ministry are my spiritual mentors, particularly my wife Lucy, who has shared this ministry with me, my children who have taught me more than they will ever realize, my colleagues in ministry throughout the years, my students and colleagues in teaching at both Wartburg and Luther Northwestern Theological Seminaries, and, though removed from me in all but memories, the people of my church in Columbus, Ohio, who provided me with my initial and continuing context for parish ministry.

1. Why Clergy Have Stress

During the airport controllers' strike of 1981, Christian Century Associate Editor Martin Marty with his characteristic tongue-in-cheek style compared the stress of controllers with that of parish pastors. Arguing that the more stressful factors in a job, the lower the work hours and higher the salary should be, he describes stress factors in the ministry of the parish pastor. Marty begins his calculations with a "typical" $33,000 annual salary and a seventy-hour work week. The pastor is called to speak the truth, incurring the danger of being run out of town. This is stress! Salary up! Hours down! As an apologist for the faith, the pastor can turn a congregant on or off through some blundering if well-intentioned word. This is stress! Salary up! Hours down! Persuading a wife beater to relinquish his gun! This is stress! Salary up! Hours down! Guiding youth groups through Bible studies and hayrides! This is stress! Salary up! Hours down!

Calculating these and other stress factors, Marty concludes that on the basis of these adjustments for stress, pastors should be paid $93,000 a year, with their work hours reduced to one hour a week!

A teacher writing to a newspaper editor during this period offered her class of eighth-graders as an example of a stressful situation. And other occupations could demand similar recognition of stress. Businesspeople, for example, are always "under the gun" in the competitive marketplace. Although a person who owns his or her own company might seem more secure than others, a friend of mine in this position finds himself under considerable stress because he feels responsible for the financial as well as vocational welfare of the people who work for him. His business decisions, therefore, affect far more than his own welfare.

As I use the term in this book, *stress* means a debilitating tension, synonymous with *distress*. Actually, however, stress is a neutral word that simply means tension. There are good stresses and bad stresses. The Canadian physician and biologist Hans Selye has done much to publicize the word and its negative effects, beginning with *The Stress of Life* (published in 1956) and in subsequent books. The title of a 1974 publication by Selye, *Stress Without Distress*, emphasizes the difference between the words. Selye further distinguishes the words with his coined word *eustress*, which means good stress. Examples of eustress are enthusiasm, eagerness, gratitude, serenity, and joy. These states are as health producing as the distresses— anxiety, depression, resentment, and frustration—are illness producing. I deal with these good stresses in later chapters. In the meantime, my use of the word *stress* is in terms of *dis*tress.

Stress can be considered a religious problem, because its presence raises questions about a person's basis for security and capacity for trust. Moreover, religion offers resources for dealing with stress. These resources are of particular significance not only for the clergy but also for the people to whom they minister.

CLERGY ARE CRISIS PEOPLE

Clergy are under stress for many reasons. First of all, clergy are crisis people. You are involved in the pains of life, the crises of life and death, more than any other helping professionals. Continuous ministry in crises can affect you deeply. When I was a hospital chaplain, in one period several people to whom I was ministering on a specific hospital floor were in agonizing pain, both physically and mentally. Day after day as I ministered to them, I could see no improvement—no relief. I went to the head chaplain and told him of my stress. When he offered to move me to another floor, I asked instead for his ministry to me in my stress so I could continue to minister to these people, to whom I now felt close.

While parish clergy may not have the hospital chaplain's concentrated ministry of visitation, they are nonetheless involved in their parishioners' crises of pain as well as in many other kinds of crises. Yet they are rarely acknowledged by other professionals as authorities in these areas. Clergy seldom even credit *themselves* as authorities.

Yet it is the clergy who deal directly with the crises of *meaning* implicit in many of these crises of pain. The clergy are involved in many of the same crises in which physicians and nurses are involved, and they continue to be involved after physicians and nurses have left the scene. They also deal with the crises of sudden death when it is too late for medical help directly. It is the clergy who most often face Job's protest—Why? Why me! Why *my* spouse? *My* child? *My* parent!

When I was a college chaplain, one of our students was hospitalized with serious burns from an explosion where he worked. When I arrived at the hospital, I was told the physician was with him. As I waited outside his room, the physician came out and motioned me to follow him to a small room that evidently served him as a retreat place. After he closed the door, he let go—with sobs that seemed to shake the whole room along with his body. "Why do things like this happen!" he cried. "That boy planned to be married in two weeks. He asked me if he would be able to make it. What do you say? He's burned too badly—it is only a matter of time!" After his sobs subsided, the physician thanked me for listening and told me I could now go to be with the student. I had seen and heard the pains of a physician—but now I had my own as well.

Clergy also deal with crises as counselors and as teachers. As counselors, however, they have the added obligation to go to people. In visitations, one never knows if and when counseling will be needed. Only good listening will reveal the need. Clergy may also be told by well-meaning persons in the congregation that certain parishioners are in trouble, but these parishioners themselves may not ask for pastoral help. What does the pastor do "when they don't come" (words that are a chapter title in a book I wrote on pastoral counseling, *How to Start Counseling*), a dilemma unique to clergy as counselors?

People in a parish find it too easy to shift their responsibilities to the pastor. "I'll tell the pastor" means "Now it's taken care of!" Parishioners absolve themselves even further by saying, "Please don't tell them who told you." So what does the pastor do? This situation is stressful. Both taking the initiative or not taking it can be wrong. And procrastination that often accompanies such dilemmas is also stressful.

The pastor's teaching ministry may also be a source of stress, focused as it often is on confirmation classes for children of junior high school age—considered perhaps the most difficult age group to teach. One of my colleagues, in reflecting over his years of confirmation instruction, commented that, in contrast to many other pastors, he never had a "smart-mouthed kid." "When I hear pastors tell about their confirmands and how they act, I think I'm lucky." He is—but he probably also is an exceptional teacher. And pastors have frustrations similar to those of other teachers over the lack of parental cooperation with their classes. Finally, the clergy's teaching ministry goes beyond the confirmation classes, and includes a variety of adult classes and in some cases senior high youth groups in the church school.

A JOB WITH A BUILT-IN COMMUNITY

Religious professionals are the only professionals whose job includes a built-in community. This community—which constitutes the second reason for clergy stress—is also an asset in many ways. The pastor's position of authority is already provided by the community structure. Pastoral authority, however, is not the same as personal authority. The latter must develop and in a sense is earned.

Moreover, the pastor's family also has an allotted place in

the community. Clergy families often realize in retrospect the advantages of this instant community when they are faced by a change in occupation with the necessity for developing their own place in a community. I left a parish ministry for a college chaplaincy and, although I had academic peers, the new situation was far different for my wife and me from the situation we had left. It took a couple of years at the college to achieve what we had started within the parish—namely, a *place* in the community.

Yet the seemingly comfortable parish community creates its own set of tensions for the clergy. Conflicts with members and conflicts between members flare up continuously. As stress analyst Hans Selye says, "the stress of living with one another still represents one of the greatest causes of distress."[1] The congregation is like a big family and, like biological families, can sometimes be racked with dissension. Churches as well as denominations repeatedly present a sad spectacle with their destructive intrafamily feuding. In our violent society at large, it is reported that most of the murders committed are of marital partners, family members, or estranged lovers. An intrafamilial ferocity, though less violently displayed, can also be experienced in churches.

The congregation is a convenient projection screen for all the individual frustrations its members experience outside the congregational community. Its organized structures are a tempting setting for the power plays and the control games so often blocked elsewhere by the impersonal structures of our society. People who have unresolved problems with authority also find a convenient outlet in attacking the vulnerable authority of the clergy. Those who are really angry at God, for example, find a logical scapegoat in the pastor's symbolic role, because it is easier and safer to attack someone who is tangibly human than to attack the Ruler of the Universe.

The congregational community can also be very supportive to the clergy and clergy family. In the pain and debilitation of physical illness and death, the congregation's support of its clergy and clergy families can be truly amazing. Yet this support has its limits. When the more sticky problems of marital strife, difficult children, or emotional illness invade the clergy family, this support can be something less than satisfactory. Here the problems come too close to the secret dreads of the lay people themselves. Clergy can talk with their parishioners about physical illness and debilitating accidents in their own family, but they rarely talk about such threatening subjects as homosexual tendencies, doubts about God, or embarrassing domestic quarrels. In such difficulties, the congregation wants the pastor to be strong for *them*, not vice versa. If the person who bears the symbol of the faith is also vulnerable in these secret areas, people may feel their own fragile hold on stability is threatened. How then can they support the pastor? Sociologist Peter Berger put it well in his advice to a young person planning to be a parish minister: "it is persons such as you who show promise of becoming what I hope to find when I go into a church—ministers who know fully the tenuousness of their performance and yet who find it in themselves to carry it on and to do so on my behalf."[2]

Conflicts that erupt in the congregation are stressful for the pastor, and if such conflicts are not managed well polarizing factions can develop in which a "we versus them" mentality disrupts the community. Clergy can also fall into this alienating mood, categorizing the congregation as *they*. The imagery then is one of "over against" rather than of "along side of," and the dynamics of a win-or-lose power struggle are set in motion. Considering others in the conflict as opponents or adversaries aggravates the conflict.

Clergy can get caught between the pressure to please people and their own anger over not succeeding. "I've worked hard in this church, and what do I get—criticism! How can this congregation be so perverse!" One of the high points in my career as a college pastor was a successful Spiritual Emphasis Week, which really captured the imagination of the students. The week climaxed with a communion service. In the midst of my elation after the event, I received a phone call from a neighboring pastor saying that several clergy in the area wanted to meet with me about a disturbing report that non-Lutheran students had received communion at the service. The issue of close Communion crops up among us Lutherans on occasion, and this was one of them. It quickly ended my elation. "We had many wonderful things happen during this week," I said, "and instead of rejoicing with us, you worry about some Methodists taking communion!" I was so angry that I refused to make an appointment.

These clergy were my constituencies in one way and in another way they were not. I could withdraw from them. But if they had been members of my congregation, I could not have withdrawn. I am so aware of this inclusiveness of the congregation that when I am a guest speaker in churches I attempt to say what the pastor might find difficult to say because he or she lives with these people day in and day out. Just recently I was speaking to an adult forum on the nuclear arms race and was meeting some opposition from those who believe our national security rests on superiority in arms. "Are there peace groups in Russia?" one man asked defiantly. I told him I didn't know. After the class, a professional lay worker in the congregation informed me that there were indeed such groups in Russia. "Why didn't you say something?" I asked. "What!" she replied—"and get my head bitten off?"

The prophetic function of the ministry (of which the preceding incident is an example) produces a built-in tension with the community. Because we in the church live also in our secular society, it is difficult and sometimes even disturbing to differentiate the values and priorities of our culture from those of our faith. The acculturation of the church is a constant danger.

In June, 1984, for example, the Southern Baptist Convention passed a resolution urging Congress to terminate the tobacco subsidy to farmers because of the health hazard tobacco presents. A North Carolina Baptist Association in the heart of

North Carolina's tobacco country strongly disagreed. One of their pastors spoke for them. "I don't look at tobacco as being a moral issue. I look at it as being a respectable product. It provides an economy for the North Carolina farmers and, quite frankly, without it my church couldn't survive."[3]

We often do not realize when this sort of "adaptation" is happening and may even resist becoming aware of it. It obviously happens to clergy as well as to laypeople, and clergy as well as laypeople may also be the prophets who help us to see that it is happening. Yet it is the clergy's appointed role in the community to be the prophet.

Few of us, however, like to be reminded of our compromise and confusion in the area of values. Naturally clergy shy away from saying what may antagonize the community in which they must live. Yet because they realize it is their duty to speak regardless of the consequences, they do not escape stress by remaining silent. And obviously they don't escape it by speaking or acting in judgment on the way our society functions. As one pastor shared with me recently, not until years after the event did he learn from his children that they had been taunted as "nigger lovers" at school because he had gone to march with the civil rights protesters at Selma, Alabama. So you have stress if you are true to your integrity and take the consequences of behaving commensurately, and you have stress if you shy away from this confrontation and become the congregation's "kept" clergy.

FRUSTRATION OVER LIVING OUT CONVICTIONS ABOUT MINISTRY

A third cause of clergy stress stems from the frustration many clergy experience in living out their convictions about ministry. The prophetic task is an example of such frustration, but the problem goes far beyond this task. Essentially the problem is a conflict over what is expected of a clergy person. The pastor may have one idea, the congregation another, and the denominational authorities may have still another.

This frustration is often expressed in a desire for privacy. As one pastor put it, "We need to distinguish between a pastoral identity and a personal identity." Clergy may feel at times that, because they have status in the congregation, the people want them and their families to live their lives in a fishbowl. Yet if there is too wide a gap between professional identity and personal identity, they can feel alienated not only from their parishioners but also from themselves. This schism is hard not only on their professional self-image but also on their personal self-image. The frustration over identity extends to the husband or wife, because the spouse also has a place in the community, if not a position, and (like corporations) congregations often want to interview the spouse of whoever is being interviewed for a call.

Denominational headquarters executives usually are former parish pastors. Their mind set, therefore, is shaped by the parish ministry. They were called to their current positions to design programs, and these programs must be carried out in the congregations. The key person for contact in these congregations, of course, is the pastor.

Depending on their morale at the moment, clergy may see in these headquarters-initiated programs just one more standard to which they must measure up. Often such new programs are introduced at denominational clergy conferences; one of my clergy friends therefore expressed reluctance to attend such gatherings. "I've got all I can do to keep up with what I'm doing," he said. "These new programs are saying that I'm not doing enough, or at least not doing it well enough." He was letting the new ways of doing things exacerbate his already nagging self-judgment.

What is "doing enough"? What are you supposed to measure up to? These questions concern expectations and decision-making authority. Who is to decide? And on what basis?

In evaluating expectations concerning the ministry, we find it difficult not to use common cultural standards to measure success, both in others and in ourselves. Questions about what constitutes success and failure are legitimate because in our faith "the last will be first, and the first shall be last" (Matt. 29:16). Yet we find it all too easy to rationalize our failures thus. For example, we may say we are failures only because we resist cultural success standards—when actually we may be unwilling to face our personal and professional deficiencies.

The conflict over expectations centers in two needs. On the one hand, we need to be in charge of ourselves and to live out our own identities in ministry. On the other hand, we need some tangible evidence of progress, of movement, of success, regardless of how we measure it. The stress created by this conflict stems from the interdependency of us clergy with our congregations and with the denominational hierarchy in evaluating our ministries. And more—we are called by God into the ministry, and to God we are responsible. Yet does God not also speak through the congregation and through the denominational hierarchy?

ADMINISTRATIVE STRESS

The conflict that clergy tend to feel concerning administrative duties is related to their frustration over not being able to fully live out their convictions about ministry. Many clergy feel that administrative details prevent them from doing what they consider to be more essential tasks, and administrative demands can in fact devour an inordinate amount of time and energy. Administration also has a low status in the pastor's theological education. Although my seminary has a large core curriculum, for example, no core course is offered in church administration. Nor is an elective course in administration taught by anyone in the pastoral department. The one elective course offered is taught by someone from outside the seminary. This lack is not unusual in seminary education but it is regrettable, because administration is really a pastoral ministry. Administration is the way the pastor, together with the lay leadership in a congregation, can provide opportunities for people to give their own talents and to receive from others.

The downgrading of administration as a legitimate pastoral ministry, however, does not create but only aggravates the administrative stress of the clergy. Since clergy, among their many roles, are managers or executive directors of their congregations, they feel the usual stress that such managers experience. Moreover, clergy work mostly with volunteers. And, unfortunately, not every layperson in a responsible congregational position fulfills that responsibility adequately. In the pastor's mind, some people seem to give their duties very little attention, simply because these duties are part of a volunteer job. Others, though very responsible may offend, by their abrasive ways, the people with whom they must work. Still others seem to resent the pastor's authority and obstruct cooperation. Although these people are in the minority in any congregation, they create a disproportionate amount of stress for the "manager." "On my bad days I envy the business world," said one exasperated pastor. "If business employees aren't doing the job, they get fired!"

The congregation is like a family, and the pastor (even a young one) is like the parent. How available can the pastor be to this huge family? Usually not as available as some pastors and laypeople might wish. When the congregation is a two- or three-point parish, as many are in rural areas, there is the added tension of one congregation feeling that another gets more of the pastor's attention. When the press of immediate demands is relaxed by having a multiple staff, as is the case in larger parishes, the potential relief in the division of labor is offset to some extent by the challenge of working together as a team, a challenge that has caused much stress for both clergy and congregations. When the senior pastor of one church with a large staff of clergy and lay workers was late for a luncheon engagement, he expressed his frustration over having spent the entire morning on personnel matters: "I never dreamed when I took this call that staff relationships could take so much time and energy!'' If one adds the rather frequent building and remodeling programs of one sort or another to the already heavy managerial load, the stress factor can intensify even more.

The time pressures of administrative demands are part and parcel of the open-endedness of the clergy's overall task. In parish ministry, the sheer number of functions other than administration is stressful in itself: preaching, teaching, counseling, pastoral care giving, training of lay ministers, nurturing, and involvement in local, national, and global concerns, as well as responsibilities in community, denominational, and interdenominational groups. In turn, time pressures can lead to family tensions. Like others, clergy tend to exploit those who are most accepting—to whom they feel the least need to prove anything—namely, their families. They assume a tolerance toward themselves from their families that they do not assume from the congregation. But this tolerance can wear thin. Spouses and children can resent the deprivation of their home life by the frequently required absence of the pastor, and they often respond with subtle hostility to the congregation.

DEADLINE STRESSES

Besides being crisis people, clergy are also deadline people. The familiar focus for deadlines is the sermon. It must not only be preached at the regularly scheduled times for services but it must also be preached to roughly the same people who probably heard the last sermon and who will probably hear the next one. These people are not strangers but people who know the preacher and whom the preacher knows. It is tough not only to come through by deadline time but to come through in a stimulating, challenging, and inspiring way to people who have already heard most of the preacher's stories and illustrations and know the particular strings that he or she tends to play. In contrast, I have it easy. As a teacher in a seminary, I only preach in our daily chapel services twice a year. In addition, I can preach the same sermon several times as a guest preacher because I preach it in different congregations.

But I've also been where the parish pastor is. I began my parish ministry the week before Lent. No graduate from a Lutheran seminary should ever be permitted to do this! No sooner did I finish the Sunday morning sermon than I had to prepare the Wednesday evening Lenten sermon. I had no "sermon barrel" of tried-and-true sermons, had to get around a new parish with no automobile, and had a new wife of two weeks. Add to this double deadline my own need to make a good first impression on my new congregation by preaching well—if not perfectly, and one has the formula not only for stress but traumatic stress. In fact, I've never gotten over it! By the next August I had already arranged for guest preachers for each of the next spring's Lenten services, at my own expense.

I can feel as badly as any other preacher about preaching a poor sermon. I feel similarly about classes that I believe I have not taught well. I don't believe that this regret is due only to perfectionist tendencies, or to an "ego trip." We preachers have a creative investment in our sermons. As Selye says, "Pride in excellence is a primeval biological feeling."[4] In addition, it is an awesome responsibility to interpret and proclaim the Word, even as it is an audacious assumption that people should listen to us speak for twenty minutes without interrupting or leaving. Although some people comfort themselves in their guilt over a poor production by saying they did the best they could, I could not comfort myself with their reassurance when I knew it was not the best that I could do. So mine was a legitimate guilt, even if my critical awareness of my carelessness came largely through hindsight.

I don't believe I'm much different from most clergy in this regard. We have a message called the Good News, which resolves guilt—but cultural values often hinder our applying it to ourselves. We participate in the usual cultural stress when we are disappointed in ourselves. And if we let the disappointment get to us, we can become mildly depressed, if only temporarily.

To avoid our own negative reaction to a poor job of preaching or teaching or whatever, we can work to improve sermons and classes in order to (among other reasons) feel good afterward. "Human emotions" says stress psychologist John Parrino, "can serve as an important source of feedback for determining the effectiveness of one's strategy for coping with life's events."[5] Feeling badly means that our strategy for coping was inadequate. Developing a better strategy leads to getting better feedback, namely *good* feelings. We "come through" for our own sakes as well as for others. We have learned—or will learn—to respect the motive of self-interest in planning priorities for time and energy; such planning reduces stress. In this sense we can learn to take care of ourselves as a necessary step toward showing care for others. In his book, *Stress Management for Ministers*, Charles Rassieur emphasizes that much clergy stress would be relieved if clergy were more concerned about taking care of themselves.

TRIBUTE TO A CALLING

I have given just some of the reasons why pastors may experience stress. Given these stresses, it is really amazing that so few cases of burnout appear among clergy. My focus in this book is on using the unique resources of our religious tradition for overcoming and preventing distress. The fact that the clergy are already using these resources for this purpose is probably the reason why less burnout appears than might be expected. I believe, however, that these resources could be used even more effectively.

Clergy stress is simply one particular manifestation of universal stress. This same stress obviously affects other religious professionals for similar reasons, because they too have a position in the same community. Consequently this book is addressed also to them. Laypeople are also afflicted with stress from the various socioeconomic, job, and family pressures on them. "Perhaps the one incontestable statement that can be made about stress," says Ogden Tanner, "is that it belongs to everyone—to businessmen and professors, to mothers and their children, to factory workers, garbagemen and writers."[6]

Although I am focusing directly on clergy stress, I am indirectly focusing also on the stress of laypeople, because clergy minister to laypeople. What we pastors learn through experience, we can most effectively communicate to others. Through the ministries of preaching, teaching, counseling, and modeling, we share the ways and means we have effectively used from our own religious resources for reducing our own stress. So while clergy stress is my emphasis, I will view it within the larger setting of the stresses that affect all people in our society, including other professional church workers. In this way clergy can see their own stress in the light of the similar stresses that are afflicting the rest of the people in the community.

Probably another reason why clergy burnout is so minimal—in spite of so much and so many kinds of stresses—is that the ministry itself is such a rewarding profession. Where else can one experience one's calling in such a variety of challenging opportunities? Where also can one have the privilege of working with people who (despite their occasional demonic ways) reveal to some extent what God had in mind when he created human beings? Where more than in the ministry can one receive the emotional rewards that come from love and affection, and from seeing at least some of the results of what the Spirit can do through one's ministry?

2. Stress Is a Killer

Why is it important to deal with stress religiously? For that matter, why deal with it at all? The answer is obvious: stress is a killer. If it is not reduced to tolerable dimensions, it can destroy us. Since religious resources are available for coping with it, they are very relevant both to clergy stress and to the stress of those to whom clergy minister.

SOME STRESS IS NEEDED—BUT NOT TOO MUCH

Paradoxically, the absence of stress can be equally deadly. People deprived of all sensation, for example, soon find the situation unbearable. Jay T. Shirley, psychiatrist at the University of Oklahoma, suspended individuals under water in a womblike tank in which they could see, hear, or feel nothing, not even the weight of their own bodies. They received air through face masks at 70°F. None could endure the experience for more than six hours.[1]

We know from our own experience that boredom—the lack of any stimulation, including stress—is indeed stressful. We human beings have what Freud called "stimulus hunger." We crave excitement—even vicariously.

Paradoxically, we even need some *distress* to adapt realistically to the events in our life. There are legitimate reasons for us to be frightened or dismayed or angered. *Not* to experience emotional distress at certain times could lead us to underestimate challenges and problems so that we maladapt rather than adapt. For example, when I fail to recognize what is demanded of me in certain speaking engagements or workshops, I become careless about my preparation. Because I experienced little apprehension beforehand, I didn't prepare adequately and consequently wasn't really ready for the actual challenge. And hospital patients who seem nonchalant before surgery are frequently the ones who are most disturbed and distressed by the actual postoperative debilitation.

Yet too much anxiety can undo us. Instead of being apprehensive and therefore mentally prepared for the ordeal, patients may become panicky and so stress their bodies that they are not ready for surgery. Or, too much anxiety about a speaking engagement can block preparation. After it reaches a certain intensity, anxiety can immobilize us.

THE PHYSIOLOGY OF STRESS

Physiologically, stress prepares us for action. The signals or stressors move our bodies to be ready for "fight or flight," to use a well-known phrase of Walter Cannon, the pioneer stress researcher of Harvard University. The first physiological response appears in the hypothalamus, in the center of the brain. This organ stimulates the emotions either of distress or eustress. The hypothalamus initiates the physiological adaptation process by its control of the autonomic nervous system, on the one hand, and by its signals to the pituitary gland, on the other. The pituitary releases the hormone ACTH (adrenocorticotrophic hormone), which in turn stimulates the adrenals to produce both the catecholamines (adrenalines) hormones and corticoids (primarily inflammatory hormones such as cortisone). Hormones are also involved in the stimulation of the autonomic nervous system, being released through nerve endings.

The combined effect of adrenal and autonomic stimulation during stress affects most of the vital organs. The heart beats faster to get more blood to the external muscles. Blood pressure rises, for the same purpose. The heart "pounds," because of the increased blood pressure. The kidneys produce increased amounts of renin. The liver pours more glucose into the bloodstream. The spleen produces more red blood corpuscles which carry oxygen to consume glucose, for the release of more energy. Blood drains from the capillaries near the skin, to prevent blood loss from wounds and to minimize heat loss. In the blood, platelets clump to prevent blood loss through clotting. In the lungs, the bronchi dilate to improve the gaseous exchange as we breathe deeper and faster. Hands and feet sweat to remove waste from the body. The pupils of the eyes dilate to sharpen sight, together with the enhancing of senses of touch, smell, and hearing. Muscles contract, ready for action.

Internally, the same hormonal combination slows down digestive activity so that more blood can be released for the body muscles that are needed for movement. Bladder and bowel muscles loosen at the same time. The thyroid gland is also activated, to increase the body's energy through increased metabolism.

All these physiological changes ready the body for strenuous action. The pattern is what Selye calls the "General Adaptive Syndrome," the biological base for what John Parrino calls the "Human Response System." So long as this physiological buildup is released in the actions of fight or flight, the response is healthy. However, when something gets stuck in the process, so that the body does not return to its normal relaxation after the stress buildup, the continuous "racing" becomes destructive. Instead of the fight-or-flight responses, the body *freezes*.

When the "motor continues to race" when stress is not released in action, the gastrointestinal lining is irritated, which can lead to duodenal and peptic ulcers. Because the stimulation also inhibits the activity of Vitamin D, needed to bring calcium into the bloodstream, osteoporosis can result. The continuous buildup of glucose in the liver can predispose the body toward diabetes. Prolonged hypertension damages blood vessels, predisposing the body to a stroke. Prolonged clumping of blood platelets leads to clots which in turn can provoke coronary thrombosis. And contracted muscles can spasm or lock, triggering pains and aches in the back, neck, and head.

Interestingly, the body's response to "good stress" is the same as to bad stress. Selye refers to this as the "nonspecific response of the body to any demand made upon it."[2] Good stress almost always leads to physical activity. Children spontaneously jump and shout, adults dance and hug. I can recall my mother being alarmed when my three-year-old daughter and a friend were so excited with the fun of being together that they kept running all over the house. "They're getting too excited," she said.

But they calmed down as their bodies tired. Good stress works that way. In bad stress, however, we may not calm down, and this intensity without an outlet may become a habit. This stress upsets what Walter Cannon considers the body's propensity for homeostasis, namely, its tendency to achieve a balance. A continued imbalance leads to exhaustion in the system, usually manifested by illness.

STRESS CONTRIBUTES TO ILLNESS

Illness caused by these stress buildups that get stuck in high gear extends far beyond the usual tension-related illnesses of migraine headaches, stomach ulcers, and muscular back pain. Research now shows that stress is a major contributor also, directly or indirectly, to six of the leading causes of death in our society: coronary heart disease, cancer, lung ailments, cirrhosis of the liver, and suicide.[3] And the combination of stress and smoking packs a lethal wallop. Fortunately, we can do something about both of these latter problems; but unfortunately, people who smoke tend to smoke more when stressed. In a study of heart attacks in middle-aged women, for example, researchers have discovered that people who smoke are five times as likely to have heart attacks. The same research showed that smoking tends to reduce the flow of blood to the brain and thus can play a role in strokes.[4]

In regard to stress alone, the Type A behavior pattern observed by researchers Meyer Friedman and Ray Rosenman is a well-recognized contributor to heart disease. Type A people are highly stressed about accomplishing much in the least amount of time. They habitually strive to prove something. Because others may block their pressure to achieve, Type A people are stressed also by hostility. Such people have three times more heart attacks than do Type B people, who are more easy-going and whose stress reactions tend to subside when no longer needed. Commenting on the role of stress on heart attacks, Selye says that all other factors involved in a heart attack only cause the danger of a heart attack; they do not in themselves precipitate an attack. "The final decisive eliciting factor is usually stress."[5] About two-thirds of all heart attack victims in the United States are men—in contrast, for example, to Mexico, where no difference between the sexes exist in this regard. This statistic obviously says something about men in our society, which I discuss in the next chapter.

Beside the illnesses in which stress can be a direct or indirect cause, stress also aggravates other diseases, such as multiple sclerosis and diabetes. This effect is probably also caused by the fact that stress interferes with the body's coping potential, its homeostatic propensity to "live" with disease. Most of us are aware, for example, that anxiety over pain increases our awareness of pain. In this sense it perpetuates and elevates the intensity of pain.

Beside maintaining high blood pressure when the person doesn't need it, and thereby straining the blood vessels, stress also raises the cholesterol level in the blood, which clogs and hardens the arteries (atherosclerosis). A study of accountants revealed that during tax collection time, their blood cholesterol level rose dramatically, as did their blood pressure and blood clotting time. Medical students showed similar conditions during their final anatomy examinations. In both instances, the conditions tended to return to normal when the pressure was off.[6] When they succeed in overcoming their behaviorial compulsions, Type A people also tend to lower their cholesterol level.

What actually seems to be happening in the continuous buildup of stress is an acceleration of the body's aging process. The stage of exhaustion in the body's General Adaptation Syndrome comes sooner rather than later. Stress results in the wear and tear of the body's "machinery." Selye attributes this exhaustion to the accumulation of undesirable by-products of the body's chemical reactions. Most of these are eliminated, but some of them are left to clog up the machinery. Specifically, these insoluble waste products include cholesterol and calcium. Calcium deposits in the arteries, joints, and the crystalline lens of the eye are examples. Blood pressure, which already tends to be high in stressed people, rises even higher to maintain circulation through the increasingly inelastic and narrowing vessels.

The younger person has an abundant supply of remaining healthy tissue with which to cope with these tissue-destroying tendencies. But as we grow older, the reserves get used up. Continuous stress accelerates the process, and losses in healthy tissue are replaced with connective scar tissues. The organs affected by stress are determined by predisposing weaknesses, just as the weakest parts of any machine break under heavy demand.

SUPPRESSION OF THE IMMUNE SYSTEM

Perhaps the most alarming effect on health is its tendency to suppress our immune system. Norman Cousins publicized this fact in his *Anatomy of an Illness*. Seriously ill with a collagen illness (inflammation of connective tissue) following a strenuous stay in Moscow, Cousins in collaboration with his physician concluded that adrenal exhaustion due to the stressful trip had lowered his resistance to a toxic substance.

Let us look at the subject religiously. The Creator has endowed our bodies with the ability to produce disease-resisting antibodies. God, in other words, is on the side of health. Stress (in terms of prolonged negative emotions) evidently interferes with this production, leaving us more vulnerable to disease. Stress, therefore, has the opposite effect from inno-culations, whose purpose is to build up the immune system. We are continually exposed to diseases; whether we become ill depends on the strength of our body's disease-resisting forces. In fact, Selye considers disease itself to be a stage of resistance to the noxious agents.

In stimulating the adrenals to release corticoids, which are primarily anti-inflammatory hormones, stress prepares the body to continue functioning when attacked, because an inflamma-tory reaction to hurt could inhibit action at the locus of the attack. However, continuous production of cortisone can pre-vent the body's disease-resisting mechanism from functioning when it should, thus reducing immune potential. These antiin-flammatory hormones repress the lymphatic organs, which produce white blood cells that play such an important defense role against disease.

O. Carl Simonton, whose Treatment Center for Cancer fo-cuses on stress-reducing practices such as meditation, says that not only may stress suppress the immune system but that, as noticed by Selye, it also tends to cause hormonal imbalances. These imbalances in turn could increase the pro-duction of abnormal (cancer) cells while at the same time sup-pressing the body's ability to destroy them. In two out of the three case histories that Simonton presents of his patients' dealing with death, their disease recurred after a period of unusual stress.[7]

Such unusual stress is often occasioned by sudden and sig-nificant losses. It has long been observed that after the death of a loved one, people are much more likely to fall sick and even die. Stress over significant loss, prolonged over weeks and months, evidently suppresses the immune system, leaving the bereaved person more susceptible to disease. The Holmes-Rahe Social Readjustment Rating Scale tabulates the events that trigger stress, and at the top of the list is death of a spouse, with the maximum numeral value of 100. Next is divorce, with 73, and then marital separation, with 65.

In these losses, people experience the gamut of negative emotions—anguish, depression, resentment, despair, and guilt. The weight of grief is so wearying that the feeling of physical exhaustion is a frequent symptom. People feel tired, fatigued, and want continuously to lie down, while at the same time finding it difficult to sleep. With their spirits "sagging," grieving people either lose their initiative or actually resist doing what needs to be done to replenish their energies. The process of recuperation seems to get stuck in the debilitating effects of a blow that hits at the very core of our being.

Although such traumatic events are highly stressful, and any combination of any stressful events occurring together could drastically increase the stress, probably just as much damage from stress is produced by everyday annoyances and hassles at work and at home. The frustration that we experience in these annoyances is essentially the thwarting of our desires. We feel temporarily out of control, both of our environment and of ourselves.

ALARMED PHYSICIANS ARE PREACHING

Physicians have become alarmed by all these devastating effects of prolonged stress. In fact, according to *Time* magazine, they are *preaching* to motivate people to take care of their bodies.[8] This is not the first time physicians have become concerned about the effect of stress on health. Probably the pioneer "stress" physician in terms of recorded history was James Johnson, who practiced in London in the early 1800s. Johnson saw a direct connection between the tensions inherent in city living and disease. Foreshadowing Hans Selye's research, he believed such tension led to premature old age.[9] And I have already referred to the research of the Harvard University physiologist Walter Cannon in the 1920s. A decade later, Adolph Meyer of Johns Hopkins University developed a "life chart" showing the relationship between disease and critical events in a person's life. This idea was later expanded by physicians Thomas Holmes and Richard Rahe who originated the Social Readjustment Rating Scale just discussed.

Stress in people's lifestyles is not the only concern alarming many contemporary physicians. They are perhaps even more alarmed about our international lifestyle. The counterpart to personal lifestyle stress on the world level is the deadly dynamic called the nuclear arms race. This concern has led to the formation of Physicians Concerned for Social Responsibility, a group of which Helen Caldecott is a leading spokesperson. There is even a chapter of this organization in Russia. Thus physicians are also resorting to preaching to bring about change in the way people live on a global level. Like the biblical prophets, they are warning of imminent doom and pleading for a change (repentance) in our international ways and in our attitudes toward national security.

Many physicians and clergy thus are obviously concerned about the same issues and involved with the same people. The needed teamwork has been painfully slow in developing, however. There has not been the rapport between the professions for each to take advantage of the other's expertise. Physicians might not have needed to resort to preaching to change self-destructive patterns if such a team had been functioning. Clergy are already skilled in preaching, both as priests and as prophets, and can benefit from an understanding of the connection between body and soul according to the physician's viewpoint. Because they have so much in common, both professions can profit from the development of an organized team.

HEALTH AND CLOSE COMMUNITY LIVING

The graduate program in pastoral care at the seminary where I teach is full time and group oriented. On one occasion a graduate student had exploratory lung surgery, and the group was quite concerned about him. He recovered so quickly from this rather drastic surgery that his surgeon asked him if he had had a support group. When he said yes, the surgeon said that he had suspected so because over years of practice he had observed that patients who had such support tended to recover more quickly. When the student shared this story with our group, we engaged the surgeon as one of our adjunct teachers.

Two research projects confirm the value of such support groups in reducing stress. At Johns Hopkins University, health records were kept for over 1,300 medical students over a period of eighteen years. The strongest prognosticator for cancer, mental illness, and suicide was discovered to be a lack of family intimacy or even a lack of resentment toward the family. The other research with 7,000 people in Alameda City, California, reported the same trend. In this project, people with few close contacts tended to die two to three times sooner than those who regularly shared with friends. These figures held up even after adjustments were made for other negative factors such as smoking and poor health histories.[10]

When people are alone and isolated, their motivation for life seems to ebb while their fears increase. This rupture of the interdependence of community living is obviously a high stress factor. Having someone to live *for* is a strong motivation to live. Conversely, cultures that practice the social ban can kill people by social withdrawal; voodoo deaths are of this character. Walter Cannon researched the social ban deaths among the Australian tribes that practice bone pointing. When the witch doctor pointed a bone at someone, the tribe considered this person as good as dead. The person *also* believed, thus contributing a kind of cooperation. And he or she soon was—the victim of an intolerable overload of stress caused by tribal rejection and withdrawal, as well as belief in the system.

Therefore, a team of physicians and clergy would necessarily (and positively) include the clergy's community, because God and church go together. The corporate nature of worship and the fellowship of believers are both expressions of the interdependence we need to keep us healthy. In the Apostles' Creed, the statement of belief in the "Holy Catholic Church" is followed appositionally by "the communion of saints." And communion is the biblical word for intimacy. Thus the image of the church as a network of interdependent members, like the members (or limbs and organs) of a human body, is a vivid metaphor for a powerful support system for health. Teamwork between clergy and physicians might conceivably be the stimulus to make this great stress-reducing potential more available. If it did nothing more than give the community a clearer understanding of the value of community for holistic health, that would provide a good antidote to privatistic penchants in religion.

STRESS AND STRESSORS

Much research into the effects of stress has concerned animals. Selye's Institute of Experimental Medicine, for example, primarily works with rats. Because animals are governed by their instincts in their response to their environment, if we disrupt their environment we also disrupt their response. Calculated changes in the environment can create sufficient stress in the animals to lead to their early deaths. For example, their intestinal tracts severely ulcerate.

Human beings are more adaptable than the lower animals because they have more than instinct to govern their response. The amount of stress that we humans experience depends on how we interpret a potential *stressor*. We too are predisposed to some extent in our interpretive processes. Heredity has its influence; so does culture. The Australian tribes interpret the pointing of the bone as death because of their culture. Yet we humans can learn to interpret these environmental stressors differently. We can be reconditioned as well as conditioned, and in contrast to other animals we can choose our own conditioning.

But our adaptability is still limited. For example, children who live on the lower floors of high-rise apartment complexes built over busy freeways seemingly adapt to the noise. Yet research has shown that they have considerably poorer reading skills than children in the upper floors, largely because they have difficulty distinguishing between similar-sounding words. The noise has had its effect even though they have apparently adapted to it.[11]

Humans, in contrast to other animals (as far as we know), are also capable of *anticipating* stress. Knowing we face an ordeal in the future can create stress for us in the present. Anticipatory stress can even go beyond the stress of the actual ordeal. It hangs like a weight on our consciousness, giving us a heavy feeling.

INTERRELATIONSHIP OF BODY, MIND, AND SPIRIT

The interrelationship within the human being of body, mind, and spirit characterizes this distinctly human form of stress. The body and the mind can become the dumping ground for the spirit's frustrations. The blocking of our personal needs undermines our mental and physical health. In his characteristic emphasis on our biological roots, Selye says we must understand the "deep-rooted biological need for completion and fulfillment of our aspirations."[12] From a biblical point of view, this need for completion is spiritual in nature as well as being reflected in our body cells.

Throughout the New Testament, this concept of completion is the projected goal of our calling and identity as children of God. The words *perfect, whole, full,* and *complete* are used interchangeably to describe this goal. The feedback that indicates we are moving in the direction of perfection is here also provided by our passions. This time they are positive; as we follow in his direction, Jesus said his *joy* would be in us and our joy would be *full* (John 15:11)

When our movement toward completion is obstructed by influences within as well as outside of us, we are thwarted in our growth. We become anxious, dissatisfied, painfully aware of our "incompletion." These feelings may form mental attitudes that harm our health. The wear and tear is further aggravated by the fact that negative emotions crowd out positive ones. Positive emotions are not only feedback on our sense of fulfillment (Selye) or on our positive adaptation to our environmental challenges (Parrino) but are also in themselves good for our overall health.

This awareness, suggested by his reading of Selye, led Norman Cousins to conduct his now-familiar laughing therapy in order to stimulate his adrenalin (adrenal hormone epinephrine). After concluding that his illness had been caused by the stress of negative emotions, which produced adrenal exhaustion and lowered his immunity, Cousins reasoned that, by the same token, positive feelings would lead to positive changes in his body. This insight initiated the treatment program he designed of watching *Candid Camera* and Marx Brothers films. And in fact not only did belly laughing reduce his pain and allow him to sleep, but it also had a positive effect on his body chemistry.[13]

One significant factor contributing to the effect that negative feelings have on our health is that they imply loss of control. Stress created by noise is a good example. Predictable, controllable noise causes less stress than noise that is not. Researchers David Glass and Jerome Singer subjected two groups of volunteers to the same amount of irritating city noises, such as clanging machinery and garbled foreign languages. While this was going on, each volunteer was given a task to do. Group A, however, was provided with pushbuttons to turn off the noise. Although almost all who had the buttons did not use them, they performed their tasks considerably better than did those in Group B. Glass and Singer suggest the key reason was that the Group A volunteers were in control, knowing they could turn off the noise whenever they desired.[14]

So the stressfulness of negative emotions, in addition to their discomfort, is that they seem to control us, rather than we them. There is no pushbutton to turn them off, and so our tolerance for their discomfort is decreased. Since we cannot control them, we have additional anxiety over when, or even whether, they will abate.

The feeling that we have lost or may lose control is a common anxiety in our culture. Urbanization and the development of megainstitutions and megacorporations give individuals a sense of having little control over their destinies. Words such as *dehumanization, impersonal bureaucracies, doublespeak,* and *big brother* reflect this loss of control. At the same time, our cultural value system continues its relentless pressure on each of us to succeed—that is, to control. Not coincidentally, people today often speak of feeling "trapped."

The preaching physicians are concerned about our response to these environmental pressures, which reflect our cultural values. I turn now to the prophetic task of evaluating these values in the light of those of the clergy's gospel.

3. Cultural Predispositions to Stress

Given the legitimate bases for clergy stress, the familiar words from the euphoric Letter to the Philippians may seem strange. "Have no anxiety [stress] about anything, but in everything by prayer and supplication with thanksgiving let your requests be made known to God. And the peace of God, which passes all understanding, will keep your hearts and your minds in Christ Jesus" (Phil. 4:6). Yet these words form the basis for what I mean by dealing religiously with stress. If there is such a thing as a biblical text for a book, this verse from Philippians is the text for this book.

NOT ENOUGH AIR TO BREATHE

Selye contends that if we could reduce the stress in people's lives we could push the average life span to a hundred years, so destructive is this tension to our health. In our culture, we tend to use tranquilizers and painkillers to cope with stress and its effects. The 1982 poisonings in which poison was slipped into Tylenol capsules revealed how many people are using this and other pain killers. While obviously not all pain is caused by stress, some is, and much pain is exacerbated by stress.

Stress is largely composed of frustration and fear, resulting from the realization that we do not control our lives. Two related words are *strain* and *worry*—both of which, in their Anglo-Saxon origins, mean "to choke" or "to strangle," "to wring" or "to constrict." In stress, we feel closed in—as though we can't get enough air, we're suffocating, or we feel "tied in knots," uptight, in spasm. If we could release this tension by screaming in panic, or shouting in rage, or crying in despair, we might feel better. But our surroundings may not reenforce us for such verbal explosions, and we would only feel guilty later for giving this "bad impression" of ourselves. This guilt in turn would add more tension. We might even be rebuked for displaying such emotion, which may leave us feeling rejected. Children can let fly with their feelings, but most people feel that adults should not—certainly not the clergy. If they do, they are "acting childish." So stress takes its toll instead on bodies, minds, and spirits.

But although it is true that becoming an adult should mean developing more mature ways of dealing with feelings, the fact is that instead of developing these more mature ways people tend to show their "maturity" by concealing feelings. Actually, the child who lets fly with feelings may be behaving more maturely than people who hold feelings in, to their own detriment. But the child's way is still not the mature way for adults. Unfortunately, people who outwardly rage as adults have the physical power to do harm to others and sometimes do.

LIBERATION OF MEN AND WOMEN

Women may be a little better off in our North American culture (relatively speaking) because they can at least cry. A recent study conducted by a psychiatric nurse at Marquette University indicates that women cry five times as much as men. In this study of 128 men and women, a distinct link was observed between regular crying and good health—which may be one reason why women live longer on the average than do men.[1] There is wisdom in the words of St. Paul, "Weep with those who weep" (Rom. 12:15). Instead, we try to get people to stop weeping. "Don't cry" is our culture's almost compulsive response to someone's tears.

U.S. men tend to hide their stress behind a macho exterior, which leaves them more vulnerable to stress-related diseases.

Boys are told, "Big boys don't cry," or "Be a man! Tough it out." All these admonitions mean "Hide the tears—the inner bleeding—and fake an opposite façade." Unfortunately, this may be wise counsel for boys, because if they show their fear or vulnerability in the school playground, for example, they may be asking for a beating by the school bullies.

How different was Jesus the man, in the Garden of Gethsemane! Facing the danger of arrest, he openly acknowledged his stress to his disciples. "My soul," he said, "is very sorrowful" (Mark 14:34). He unapologetically asked for their support, because he needed it, and took them to the garden to be with him in his ordeal. "Remain here and watch," he said. When they went to sleep instead, he awakened them, saying, "Could you not watch with me one hour?" (Matt. 26:40). Earlier he wept with the weeping Mary.

It is significant that Jesus was an Eastern man. In the same Eastern world, Job's three friends came together "to comfort and condole with him" in his pain. In other words, they came as pastoral caregivers. When they had difficulty recognizing him because of his emaciation, they wept and wailed with him because "they saw that his sorrow was very great" (Job 2:12–13). They assumed that this nonverbal communication of compassion was sufficient, so that they had no need to speak for seven days and seven nights. This kind of abandon would be unlikely among Western men; the culture has other expectations of men and of pastors.

Most clergy are men and share the problems of other males in our culture regarding their feelings. But if current seminary enrollments are any indication, this preponderance of men in the ministry is going to change. Women are already bringing their feminine freedom with feelings into the ministry. The ministry itself will thus be changed accordingly.

The Western man (especially the North American man) is not the way he is because he is a man, however, but because of a cultural distortion of what it means to be a man. Men in our culture are deprived of their rights, as are women, although the deprivation is different. Men are deprived of their right to be open and vulnerable. They are pressured to look strong and to act as if they "have it all together." We need feminists to battle for women's rights; and we also need *masculinists* who will fight for the liberation of maleness from its cultural stereotypical prison. Men in our culture need help, and need also to be free enough to admit it and even more free to ask for it.

Of course, women are not as free to be open as may appear from the study on crying. Middle-aged and older women in particular use large amounts of tranquilizing drugs; they have a high incidence of depression. A woman pastor who ministers mostly to this age group of women says she frequently hears someone say, "I can't go unless I take my Valium." White women are more likely than men to take Valium and other mild tranquilizers; men who do take them are almost as likely as women to take them for extended periods.

Fortunately, the use of Valium is declining, perhaps partly because physicians are more wary about prescribing it. Another reason may be that women now entering midlife have been influenced by the women's liberation movement and are more assertive. One major factor involved in depression is the repression of aggressive feelings such as anger.

Naturally, the one emotion considered "negative" that men are permitted to express (anger), women in our culture are pressured *not* to express. It is not considered "ladylike" or even "feminine" to express anger or even to act aggressively. Nancy Kasselbaum, one of the two women Senators at present, entered the U.S. Senate after twenty-five years as a full-time homemaker. From her experience in both worlds, she says, "I've always thought that a woman has a very tough time. A woman can't appear to be too aggressive or you become a threat to men and women."[2] Since "anger turned inward" is one cause of depression, middle-aged and older women may be more susceptible, because their culture has denied them the right to be overtly angry. So the covert rage within undermines their self-image and debilitates their energy and spirit.

Science writer Maggie Scarf believes that the predominance of depression among women (two to six times as much as among men, she says) is caused by their proportionately greater need for emotional bonding with others. In our time ruptures of these relationships have increased phenomenally. These ruptures, coupled with the liberation pressures on women to be independent, says Scarf, account for this disproportionate amount of depression.[3]

Some people believe the high incidence of depression among women is caused by the facts that women tend to go to physicians more than do men, and that the physicians to whom they go tend to be *men*, who in turn think women need tranquilizers. Others believe that the figures do not take into account the high incidence of alcoholism among men, in which depression is often a factor. But regardless of how one interprets statistics, it is indisputable that both men and women are under pressure from our cultural value system regarding their gender roles and need liberation to be who they really are as human beings.

THE DREAD OF LOSING

The cultural distortion of masculinity and femininity reflects a cultural distortion of what it means to be a human being. Former President Lyndon Johnson's father supposedly aroused his son from bed in the morning by saying, "Get up, Lyndon, or everybody in the neighborhood will have a head start on you." The pressure is on! From childhood onward, you are in a competitive rat race in one way or another; and if you lose out, you're considered a loser as a *person*. Whether the pressure is to be a sex symbol or an athlete, boys and girls enter into a world in which "how they compare" determines more than the particular comparison—it determines their worth as people.

So every obstacle in your way to being a winner is more than an obstacle—it may directly threaten your worth as a person, your self-esteem. The risks are high in the competitive comparative milieu because your *personhood* is at stake. If you lose our here, you may really feel lost!

I have often heard clergy comment about the competition that exists in their own pastoral conferences. When people have their guard up, they do not share much—whether clergy or lay. If my fellow pastors are also my competitors, I find it hard to rejoice in their reports of success even as I find it hard to share with them my vulnerabilities and failures. This same guardedness also characterizes congregations where the nice clothes that people feel they must wear to attend worship match the nice countenances they feel they must "put on." Although tears may be in their hearts, their faces smile.

The frustration we feel over obstacles is based on a deep-seated dread that we won't "make it." The implied imperative "You must!" generates its own doubt: "What if I don't?" The fear of this possibility may already judge us. We don't prepare for failure consciously, but we may be doing so regardless. And the fear of failure does not always spur us to succeed—it can also pull us down toward destruction. In *Concept of Dread*,[4] Kierkegaard developed the thesis that the dread of sin may actually lead us into sin. Such fears work negatively on our self-image. The imprint of guilt only adds to the lure of failure—it is really what we fear we deserve.

The labels we put on ourselves in our inward musings have a lot to do with how we behave toward ourselves and others. So the question you need to ask is "How do you 'stamp' yourself?" If you envision yourself primarily as "heavy" or "small" or "uncoordinated" or "physically unattractive" or "poor" or "intellectually inadequate" or relatively ungifted compared to most others in your profession, you are seeing yourself as disadvantaged, according to our culture's priorities. Intellectually, rationally, and logically, you may not believe that these qualities or others are really debasing to your personhood. And, of course, they are not. Even more, they are not synonymous with your person.

But because our culture identifies them as the marks of a pariah, rationality may cave in before this onslaught on our self-image. We then reach out to claim these negative judgments as though we were perversely attracted to them. And our feelings follow this attraction. The woman who is depressed because she believes she is physically unattractive, although other people see her as attractive, for example, is not uncommon.

The whole process can be too much for our logic. As someone has said, "The fish is in the water, and the water is in the fish"—we are reared in our culture, and our cultural values become part of us. This is the predisposition behind Transactional Analyst Eric Berne's concepts of the life script and the injunction. We live out our own marks and labels as though we were following a preordained script, or obeying an injunction by an unseen authority.

CHALLENGING THE CULTURAL DISTORTIONS

To deal religiously with stress, we need to begin by challenging the cultural distortions of what it means to be a human being. This is the prophetic task. As the light of the world, the salt of the earth, the conscience of the community, the church needs also to recognize the difference between (1) its values and priorities as the Body of Christ and (2) the values and priorities of the culture in which it exists. The distortion of what it means to be human is the spiritual basis of our stress. Our "interpreter" is out of whack because it has copied these culturally accepted interpretations despite their distortion. These interpretations of the human being constitute a cultural creed of what constitutes personal value.

This cultural creed is the antithesis of the Christian creed. Our compulsive copying of it, however, is not achieved without conflict. We are aware, though feebly, that our culture is wrong in its assessment of human worth, but this awareness leads mainly to inner confusion. Jesus said that his followers are "in the world" but not "of the world." How can one be *in* but not *of*—function in the world of distorted values and priorities and yet not internalize them?

From practical experience, remaining thus committed seems impossible. We live with duplicity. Yet we can change this duplicity—at least some of the time. When we see through the distortions, a truer picture of human worth replaces it. Then we experience basic liberation, namely, liberation from the notion that our worth must be proved. Jesus said he had come to "proclaim release to the captives" and "to set at liberty those who are oppressed" (Luke 4:18). All other liberations depend on this basic liberation from the guilt over simply being who we are. The Good News that Jesus preached offers a better way out of this bondage than do the never-ending demands of the competitive-comparative battlefield.

To build his behavior model of "altruistic egotism" for reducing stress, Hans Selye replaces the biblical direction of "loving your neighbor as yourself" with "earning your neighbor's love."[5] I believe that in doing so he is succumbing to the norms of our culture, which are inherently stress producing. I don't see much difference between *earning* and *proving*. As a counselor, I have often attempted to help people escape from the bondage to conformity that grew out of a longstanding warning; "If you do that—or don't do this—people won't like you."

Selye's objection to loving your neighbor as yourself is that it is impossible. To demonstrate this, he changes the text to read, "Love your neighbor *as much as* yourself." I feel this change not only alters the words and meaning of the original text but it also changes the motif for one of quantity. In doing so, he has radically altered the biblical meaning of love.

The biblical word for love in this directive is the Greek word *agape*, which by its very nature *cannot* be earned. While it includes the other meanings of love, *agape* also transcends them. In contrast to these other meanings, *agape* provides its own stimulus for loving. Therefore it offers a security that no other kind of love can offer.

In reality, can *any* kind of love be fully earned? Friendship love, for example, involves a personal attraction of "chemistry" of one person for another. Eros love depends on a physical or sexual attraction. What *can* be earned is admiration for character or respect for competence. But love? How does a baby earn love? By being a cute baby? A "good" baby? What happens when a baby is neither cute nor "good"?

Love to provide the security we need to resist stress, must be *unconditional*. This is how God loves us. As social activist William Sloane Coffin puts it, "God's love doesn't seek value, it creates it."[6] We are more likely to become lovable if we are loved than if we are trying to prove ourselves worthy of it. As we received *agape* from God, we can extend it to ourselves and then love our neighbor with this same *kind* of love. One can give what one has received.

Dealing religiously with stress thus means breaking the chains that bind us to stress-producing values. It means affirming a radically different understanding of human worth, in which the distinctions of *winner* and *loser* have no meaning.

The liberating influence of this Good News has something to do with why we get up in the morning. Rather than awakening to the pressure to get moving before someone gets ahead of us, we can greet the new day with the joy of being, because nothing has to be proved. Arise then, for "this is the day which the Lord has made: let us rejoice and be glad in it" (Ps. 118:24).

4. Stress in Our Work

Stress tends to focus on one's job. Marty's parody of the stress of parish pastors and air traffic controllers, with which I introduced Chapter 1, is a takeoff on this fact. We could expect this focus, because our cultural values also tend to focus on the job; the job is the major way by which our culture evaluates us. It is no coincidence, for example, that stress and stress-related illnesses are increasing in women as more women enter the job market for work outside the home.

And the clergy are experiencing stress in their job not unlike the stresses the people in the congregation are experiencing. Consequently, as clergy deal with their own job stress they are building the understanding they need to help minister to others. So while I focus on clergy job stress in this chapter, I also examine job stress in general, so that the immediate problem can be seen within the larger context to which it belongs.

I often encounter objections when I refer to the ministry as a *job*. It is a *calling*, I'm told. Actually, *all* legitimate occupations are callings, and all God's people can look on their jobs in this light. In reality, we are called as *persons*. Our jobs are one way in which we live out this calling. A friend of mine "left the ministry" to become a personnel director for a large corporation. He is continually asked why he left the ministry. "I never left it," he says. "I'm still in it." He hasn't even left his occupational stress. "The stresses are still there," he says, "but in a different setting."

Given the focus on jobs as a measure of personal value, it should not be a surprise that unemployment would lead to unemployment blues. Losing one's job can mean losing one's basis for personal worth. I can recall seeing this effect of unemployment on my father during the Great Depression. He was a teller in a bank that folded. A new bank was opening, but not all the former employees would be rehired. Each morning my mother encouraged him to go to the bank and make himself visible. Although I was only a child, I could see and feel how difficult and demeaning it was for him to do so.

Our society has changed much since the Great Depression. Many people have known little more than a welfare survival, and the meaning of a job for them is not the source of pride that it is for those reared on the work ethic. This is not always because they don't prize a job, but because they can't get a job. Changes in sex roles no longer make it a source of humiliation for a man to live off his wife's income. Some people presently unemployed are not so identified with having jobs that they cannot adjust to being without one. Yet the old job-determines-worth ideology is still endemic to our culture, and many people find the lack of a job as ego deflating as my father did.

Some laypeople are surprised to hear about clergy unemployment. Yet in most denominations other than Roman Catholic more clergy exist than there are clergy positions to fill. Some of our seminary graduates wait one or two years before receiving a call—after eight years of preparatory education.

Moreover, although they have a great deal of higher education, clergy lack the job skills needed for employment outside the church. Our seminary faculty believes our students should learn another job skill so that they will not be trapped into unemployment if ministerial positions are lacking. And some clergy, dissatisfied with the ministry, believe they would be happier in a secular job. My counsel to them is not to resign their position until they actually have another job. It may be stressful to stay where they are, but prolonged unemployment or underemployment is even more stressful.

POTENTIAL FOR UPWARD MOBILITY

Jobs are usually evaluated in terms of their potential for upward mobility—for getting ahead. Positions without such potential are termed "dead-end jobs." Government-financed jobs to relieve unemployment, for example, have been opposed on the basis that such jobs are dead-end jobs. Presumably a dead-end job is worse than no job. The problem with upward mobility in the job picture is that there is little room at the top, and the middle gets awfully crowded, and the bottom is always within threatening distance. Still, this ladder-climbing syndrome continues to dominate the job mind-set while competition puts on the pressure.

I know of a young pastor, bright and capable, who is serving a congregation that really should be part of a two-point parish. But the congregation understandably wants a pastor all to itself, although they really cannot afford it financially. As a result, instead of getting at least a cost-of-living raise, he gets annual salary cuts, until he is now well below the denominational guidelines for seminary graduates in their first year of ministry. He and his family are not physically starving, since their farmer parishioners are generous with their products, but the situation is hard on his professional self-esteem.

Another pastor approaching midlife is serving a three-point parish. "I really don't think this is where I should be at this point in my career," he said.

Under such pressure, we are obviously concerned about our image. How do the VIP's see us in terms of job market ability? Protecting this image becomes very important. Pastors, for example, are reluctant to go to their bishops for counsel—despite the fact that a bishop is supposedly the pastor's pastor. They are afraid they would jeopardize their chance for "advancement"—or, as we clergy would put it, for a better call.

So long as we conceal our hurts and needs, we remain at least nominally in control. But we surrender this control when we reveal ourselves to one another. Then we must trust, not only ourselves but each other. I grew up with the aphorism, "What you don't say won't hurt you." Or, what you don't say, you don't have to wish later that you could take back. But if we think of our need for personal help, it is a different story.

Søren Kierkegaard tells of the emperor who was caught in this dilemma. The emperor needed to talk about his troubles so that he would feel better. Yet he did not want anybody to know that much about him lest they use this knowledge against him or lest he feel embarrassed in their presence. He "resolved" the dilemma by confiding in slaves and then having them executed.

When women were first permitted to be ordained in my church, they had a difficult time being placed in congregations and still do. The resistance was and is not only theological but psychological. Many congregations are reluctant to have a woman pastor because of their past familiarity with an exclusively male clergy. Also, some male clergy are reluctant to relate to women as peers in religious understanding and authority. Despite such resistance, women usually do receive calls, but most often as assistant pastors serving under male seniors. The problem now concerns a woman pastor's second call or change of pastorate. The issue is upward mobility: will women be able to ascend the ecclesiastical ladder—particularly when this means that some men may have to relate to women as *their* seniors?

We need a challenge in our jobs, because unless a job challenges our abilities and creative capacities it soon becomes boring. And some times we believe we have given a job all that we have and it is time to move on. In either case, we need work that offers more opportunities. In times of unemployment, unfortunately job mobility is frequently not available, and the resulting frustration only adds to the stress.

The pressure for upward mobility, however, comes not only from the need for more challenging opportunities, but also from the need to prove our worth as persons. When you are the victim of unemployment, what happens to this sense of worth that comes from the "better" job? In most instances, it deteriorates. A symptom of the ensuing demoralization is the increase in spouse and child abuse as well as chemical dependency among the families of the unemployed.

STRESS INCREASES AS CONTROL DECREASES

With so much at stake in our jobs, it is little wonder that jobs with the greatest stress are those where the worker has the least control over how things operate even though he or she is responsible. An O'Hare Airport study of air traffic controllers, completed just prior to the controllers' strike, confirmed the high stress level of the job, but not simply because these controllers have to make decisions that affect the lives of others. They are stressed also because, although they are called *controllers*, they often feel they are anything *but* in control because of fluctuating weather, pilot error, and equipment failure.

So also nurses have more stress than physicians because they have less control while still having the responsibility. People in middle management experience more stress than either those of upper or lower management for the same reason. They are in a squeeze from the top and the bottom. Clergy are like middle management, in that they are squeezed by their congregations and by their denominational hierarchy as they attempt to follow the Spirit.

Jobs in which one may encounter severe conflicts with fellow workers or supervisors are high-stress jobs. Again, these conflicts block one's control over situations for which one is responsible. A good example, again, is the parish pastor, who depends on the cooperation of congregational leaders on a voluntary basis to carry out his or her desired programs of ministry. As a politician who is also a lay leader in a congregation put it, "In politics if you get 51 percent of the votes you are *in* as much as if you got 90 percent. In the congregation if you get 51 percent of the votes you are immobilized."

Another example is the school teacher. Teachers need the cooperation not only of students but also of parents and school administrators. Many teachers feel, for example, that in matters of discipline they get little if any support from either parents or administrators. I know of one high school teacher who sent two students home from a school trip because they were using drugs. It had been understood beforehand that the parents of such students would pay the transportation costs if such should occur. In this instance, the parents refused to do so. When the teacher persisted, the principal backed down under the parental pressure and paid the fares out of a school fund—for the sake of public relations, he said.

It is hard to avoid such conflicts, because institutions seem to breed them. When we first begin a job, it may seem as if we were working for the ideal institution (company, store, plant, agency, or church). But honeymoons have a way of wearing off, and the warts begin to show, or some of the ogres become visible. Then perhaps our paranoia sets in. As studies have shown, we tend after a time to believe that we are giving more to the job than we are receiving—certainly more than others in the institution seem to recognize or appreciate.

Institutions also have a way of corrupting people. We may do things as "institutional people" that we would not do as individuals. This is also true for church institutions. Church councils, boards, or sessions, for example, can make cruel decisions, though each member as a person would not act cruelly. They can be as lacking in compassion and as ruthless in their deliberations as a profit-greedy corporation.

Moreover, much conflict with others in our jobs is "underground." For example, Bob was a seminary intern whose curriculum required that he spend a year in a congregation under the supervision of the pastor. It wasn't long before Bob sensed that the pastor was displeased with him. But the pastor said nothing, so Bob could not figure out what he had done wrong. And because he had a room in the parsonage, he could not escape from the tension. As Bob began to discover, the pastor showed his displeasure by becoming silent even with his family. "Why can't he say it when he doesn't like what somebody is doing!" Bob said with exasperation. He finally confronted the pastor when his intern year was nearly over. Then the pastor reluctantly informed him about a careless act that Bob had committed early in his internship.

Lack of candor and openness accounts for much unnecessary interpersonal stress. If Bob had been free to move, he would have. Surely there must be a better supervisor, a better place to work, a church with more understanding people, a more ideal institution to work for! Bob probably could find a better institution but not a perfect one. Perhaps he also could have confronted the pastor sooner.

UNFAIR ADVANTAGES

Adding to job stress are what we may see as unfair advantages in the competitive milieu. Rather than having fair competitive standards based on competence as the way of determining "who gets the job" or "who gets ahead," personal charm or influence may put someone on the "inside track." Such events take away our control. Other unfair advantages—such as discrimination because of sex, race, religion or age—also take away our control.

For example, in the city in which I grew up, a Catholic friend of mine got a job after college with a local business. I knew one of the vice presidents of the company and asked him if he knew my friend. "Oh yes," he said. "He's got a lot of ability. Too bad that he is of the wrong religion. Otherwise he would go places in our company." Thank God this kind of discrimination seems to belong more to our past than to our present, but it does still exist.

One form of discrimination that we are just beginning to challenge in the job market is discrimination by chronological age. A good place to start fighting ageism is in the church. I don't know of any professional who is more discriminated against because of age than the parish pastor. One older pastor once sat across from me in my office, waving a letter. "Read this," he said. "Dear Pastor," the letter began, "We thank you for the interview we had with you regarding the call to St.

John's Church. From all that we can determine you are an excellent preacher, a good pastor with the youth and also appreciated by the aged. Your reputation in pastoral care is outstanding, and you appear to be an efficient administrator. Unfortunately, however, we believe that at fifty-nine, you are too old for our congregation."

He shrugged in frustration. "Don't they realize that I'm able to give them so much more *because* I'm fifty-nine years old? When I think of what I've learned about pastoral ministry in the last thirty-four years—in fact, in the last ten years—"

His voice trailed off, and he looked beyond me, lost in the scope of his last remark. He was a pastor who should have been confident and secure in his work in view of his track record in the ministry. Yet he looked crestfallen and defeated. "I could sue them," he said, coming back to me. "But I won't. It's just not my nature."

I recently talked with a former student about his experience in the ministry. "My first parish was tough," he said. "Through the help of the bishop, I was finally able to move. The next parish was just the opposite. I like it so well I stayed ten years. Even then I only moved because I thought it best for the congregation to have a change. My present parish is just like the second one. I said to my wife the other day, 'I'd like to stay here ten years also.' She gasped. 'Tom,' she said, 'Do you realize that in ten years you'll be fifty—nobody will want you then.' " She's probably right! So here he is at forty stressed over the ageist discrimination that awaits him in the not-too-distant future.

In the same culture in which a pastor is considered too old at fifty-nine to receive a call to a parish commensurate with his abilities, we elect a man to the Presidency of the United States at age seventy who never had the job before. The voters of Mississippi did not consider John Stennis too old for another six-year term in the U.S. Senate at age eighty-one, and they reelected him overwhelmingly. Yet people in much less demanding jobs are made to feel too old for the job when only in their sixties.

Even Ronald Reagan did not completely escape ageist discrimination. In his column in the *Washington Post*, David S. Broder, discussing conflicts in the national government, referred to the protagonists as "septuagenarians Ronald Reagan and Tip O'Neill." I reminded Broder by letter that although Howard Baker's name appears in the same column, he did not refer to Baker in terms of his age. Why the discrimination? His reply was that he used *septuagenarian* to indicate that people who are doctrinaire are less likely to change views at that age than earlier. I'm sure he did not realize that even his defense smacked of ageism. Obviously he used the term *septuagenarian* to convey a negative impression.

Although the mandatory retirement age has been placed at seventy by the government, too many companies begin phasing their employees out before this time. Using demeaning, demoting, and other harrassing tactics, they hope to "persuade" people who are approaching this age to retire sooner. The law forbids actually retiring such people before age seventy, but it doesn't prevent them from shifting such people to other jobs where they have little to do or little importance in the company structure.

Parish pastors usually have no compulsory retirement age, but they feel the same pressure regardless, and few even wait until seventy to retire. This tendency is probably partly due to the fact that they often have the option of becoming visitation pastors in large congregations on a part-time basis or of serving on an interim basis in churches temporarily without a pastor.

Unfair discrimination such as sexism and ageism as well as other sources of job stress can drain our energy. The resultant state of fatigue is a common symptom of stress. Energy is an interesting possession. It has the capacity to expand or to diminish depending on the attitude within which it is used. How we interpret what we see, or how we envision what we anticipate, determines to a great extent the amount of energy we will have. If we are positive rather than apprehensive about our task, hopeful rather than skeptical about the outcome, and feel supported by others rather than attacked, we are likely to have more energy for *doing* than would be the case were our perceptions reversed.

Each negative interpretation produces its own stress. For example, you may have noticed that you can get up in the morning feeling rather energetic, and then you begin to reflect on all the stressful things you have to do that day. And before you realize it, your energy is gone and you feel fatigued enough to go back to bed. Obviously energy comes partially from our *heads*. The way you interpret a situation determines the energy you can bring to it.

Energy in this context is actually eustress. It is the passion for doing. And it is this *eu*stress—this energy—of which *dis*-tress drains us.

5. The Eye of Faith

Although there are plenty of reasons for stress—all sorts of obstacles to the fulfillment of our goals—these reasons alone are not sufficient to *distress* us. St. Paul understood this. "We are troubled on every side," he informed his Corinthian congregation, "but not distressed" (2 Cor. 4:8 AV). Why not? Because he believed in the providence of God. Coping religiously with stress means coping with it from the vantage point of this belief.

AS GOD OR UNDER GOD

At the risk of oversimplifying, I believe we can approach any present moment in basically two ways. One is to approach it *as* God—as though all depended on me or on resources I (as God) can control. The other is to approach it as *under* God, in which I can trust a higher power. I take these differentiating terms from the story of the fall in Genesis, in which the tempter's ploy in the seduction is the promise that in eating the forbidden fruit, Adam and Eve would be *as* God.

The Christian faith clearly distinguishes between the creature and the creator—between human beings and God. This division—rather than that between the natural and supernatural—is emphasized. Søren Kierkegaard saw in the creature's attraction to bridging this gap the corrupting influence within all human enterprises. "Christianity," he said, "keeps watch to see that the deep gulf of qualitative distinction between God and man be firmly fixed."[1] The tower of Babel (Gen. 11:4–9) is a symbol of the human desire to leave below the limits of creatureliness and to penetrate into the heavens wherein we believe are the unlimited potentialities of divinity.

I spent a sabbatical year researching (through personal

involvement) what is loosely called the human potential movement, and profited both professionally and personally from
the workshops, marathons, and encounters of the various
expressions of this movement. When religion entered the picture on these occasions, however, it tended to blur this distinction between humans and God, probably because of the
movement's attraction to Eastern religions. Simplistic adap-
tions of Eastern thought in the movement are illustrated in the
following blurb of a human potential promotional flyer: "The
thinker in all of us manifests whatever it believes to be true.
Within the dominion of our minds we are surely God. For we
can control what we think, and what we conceive to be true
becomes the Truth." When I mentioned the word *God* in a
discussion with one of the leaders of such a workshop, he
responded in a similar way. "Who is God?" he asked. "I am
God. You are God. We are God."

Sometimes Christians seem to say something similar. Athanasius, the great spokesperson for the incarnation in the creedal
controversies of the fourth century, said, "He (God) indeed
assumed humanity that we might become God."[2] Even the
New Testament contains some of this language. The Second
Epistle of Peter, for example, says that through God's "pre-
cious and very great promises" we "become partakers of the
divine nature" (2 Pet. 1:4). The Epistle to the Ephesians puts
it even more strongly, in its prayer that we "may be filled with
all the fulness of God" (Eph. 3:19).

But these are metaphorical expressions for the "indwelling"
of God's Spirit made possible by the mediation of Jesus the
Christ, and are based on the assumption that an infinite distinction always exists between God the creator and the people
whom he has created. While the divine Spirit is within us, it
is in dialogue with, not identical with, our spirit. Jesus "did
not count equality with God a thing to be grasped, but emp-
tied himself . . . being born in the likeness of men" (Phil. 2:6–
7). He was the distinct—the unique—incarnation, "the image
of the invisible God" in whom "all the fulness of God was

pleased to dwell" (Col. 1:15, 19). Through his mediation, we are reconciled—made one with God. This oneness that we have with God is a bond created by his unconditional love. It is as different from the human desire to be *as God* as forgiveness is from sin. Being a receiver of his forgiveness places us *under* God.

Therefore if I approach any present moment *as God*, I must be in control, or I lose my divine identity. However, if I approach it *as under God* I can live without this control, if necessary, because I believe that ultimately this control lies with God. If I approach life as God, I tend to demand perfection, particularly of myself, and find it difficult to put anything aside that is not satisfactorily completed—and then I tend to project these same demands others, particularly on members of my family.

Such projected demands are essentially judgments we lay on others. Unless these others come up to these perfectionist standards, they are implicitly convicted of failure—not only in their pursuits but also in their persons. At times this judgment may also be explicit. I know of a father who refuses to be reconciled to his daughter because she has offended him by deviating from his moral standards for behavior. When a friend tried to mediate between them and suggested to him that even God forgives, his reply was "But I am not God." Yet in withholding the forgiveness that he could have given, he was acting as though he *were* God.

If I approach any present moment as under God, I can accept the limits of my creatureliness. Since I know I can't have it all, I can enjoy what I *have*, instead of being frustrated over what I do *not* have. This stance toward myself helps me to allow others, particularly those in my family, to be who they are.

THE LONELINESS OF BEING AS GOD

Being as God can be a very lonely existence, which adds to the stress. In fact, loneliness is a stress in itself and the wide prevalence of loneliness is our culture is a major source of our stress. Independence, rather than interdependence, is the American ideal. This emphasis corresponds to the American emphasis on individualism rather than on corporateness. We tend to see ourselves as independent units—as the individual whole—rather than as parts of the larger whole. In contrast, the Christian emphasis is on the *body* of believers, with each person as an interdependent member of this body. Families are also parts of this body—which is actually the larger or extended family we need for support.

In contrast, our culture has produced the nuclear family with parents and children as an isolated unit, supposedly sufficient in itself not only for survival but also for its own development. It is no coincidence that the family—along with other institutions in our society—is in trouble. All of us—individuals, couples, families—need to see ourselves, experience ourselves, as integral parts of a community in which the dynamics of interdependence—mutual giving and receiving—provide the needed stress-reducing support. When we share our troubles with others, our burdens become lighter. We feel better even if the troubles themselves are not resolved. Through such support, we are able to carry on. Obviously, we humans function best when we are interdependent members of a community. In fact, it is precisely this interdependence that makes community possible.

Interestingly enough, the more a stressful event is shared, the less each person appears to be stressed. A good example is the eruption of Mount St. Helens in the state of Washington. One would think that this eruption, which buried people as well as homes, would increase the stress of people who live in the area. Yet the mental health institutions in the area actually reported a drop in their clientele during this period. The explanation offered is that although local people were certainly not in control of events, they were in the events *together*. They felt some excitement in the shared danger. Besides, it is hard to get angry at a volcano.

The same is not true, however, in man-made calamities, such as the despoiling of the environment due to chemical poisonings (as at Love Canal in New York or at Times Beach in Missouri) or to leaks from nuclear power plants (as at Prairie Island in Illinois or Three Mile Island in Pennsylvania). Although the trauma in these instances was shared by the whole community, the individual stress level continued high. One explanation is that these calamities were related to *human* greed, negligence, or error. We rage against *people* who endanger us and our children in their pursuit of profits. And rage itself is stressful. Beside anger, it contains both loneliness and fear. In addition, the diseases that may afflict us because of such poisonings do not immediately show up. They may strike this year or in twenty years or never, and they may afflict children as yet unborn. Such nebulous anticipation is stressful, particularly when the disease may be as feared as cancer is. Although the affliction is shared with members of the community, it is also a humanly caused affliction. Anger over the cause seems to outweigh the stress relief of sharing.

Creatures can share each other's burdens; gods have a hard time doing so. Since the Garden of Eden, we have been impatient with the limits of our creatureliness, trying instead to be as God. And we are just not up to it. Stress is the inevitable result of this human identity crisis.

The defensiveness that often inhibits us in developing our personal relationships largely originates in this reluctance to own up to our creaturely limits. With knee-jerk predictability, we react defensively when confronted with or even gently reminded of our limitations and fallibilities. This defensiveness is almost impenetrable, simply because it is so habitual. Our only safety seems to be in concealing our vulnerabilities and limits from observation. But the continual threat of exposure makes for a stressful existence, leading to less and less intimacy and more and more loneliness.

We clergy also can become defensive when reminded of our shortcomings or even limitations, as some church councils have found out. Like others in their job situations, we tend to believe that we are giving to the congregation more than we are receiving. At times we can feel disgruntled, unappreciated, convinced that neither the hierarchy nor the congregation recognizes our true value. So any implication from the church council or other committees or people that more ministry needs to be done or that what is being done is not adequate, may raise our hackles. Before we realize it, we may react abruptly or even sharply, leaving the often unintentional critic somewhat taken back.

HOW WE INTERPRET

Clearly, the way in which we view our limits has everything to do with how they affect us. And whether we are stressed by any present *moment* depends to a large extent on what we see in that moment. In his short story *"Goodbye My Brother,"* John Cheever laments over someone who sees only the negative:

"Oh what can you do with a man like that? What can you do? How can you dissuade his eye in a crowd from seeking out the cheek with acne, the infirm hand; how can you teach him to respond to the inestimable greatness of the race, the harsh surface beauty of life; how can you put your finger for him on the obdurate truths before which fear and horror are powerless?[3]

In another of Cheever's stories, *"The Common Day,"* a wife had been trying for years to persuade her husband to buy an abandoned farm homestead. They had visited many such places to no avail but her hopes were still high as they visited "the Emerson place." When they arrived to view the old homestead, neither of them spoke. Cheever writes, "Where she saw charm and beauty, he saw advanced dilapidation and imprisonment."[4]

And in his autobiography, *Once to Every Man*, William Sloane Coffin recounts the story of his divorce while chaplain at Yale University. It took place in a time when divorce among clergy was not as accepted as it is now, and Coffin was prepared to resign. To his surprise, Kingman Brewster (Yale's president) refused to accept his resignation. He and Brewster had not been seeing eye to eye on Coffin's controversial activities, and the resignation could have been a convenient way for Brewster to rid himself of his troublesome chaplain. Instead, he invited Coffin to move in with him and his wife.

Still not satisfied that he should not resign, Coffin talked it over with his faculty colleague Richard Sewall. Sewall also advised against resignation and gave him a compelling reason. "Bill," he said, "If you have suffered from anything, it is from an aura of too much success. A little failure in your personal life can only improve your ministry." The difference between the two lay in how each viewed the effects of this trauma. Reflecting on the situation, Coffin writes, "Of what was I so afraid? Of failure itself. I had never been taught how to deal with failure—not really. Rather, I had been groomed to succeed, and since childhood I have been pretty lucky. And beyond personal failure, to fail as a Christian minister, to be a Christian minister who couldn't keep his own marriage together—that was a possibility too threatening to contemplate."[5]

Coffin goes on to describe how he interpreted his parenting role during this ordeal and how the subsequent years helped him to see things differently. "I rather pridefully assumed," he wrote, "that whatever problems they (the children) were having could only be caused by shortcomings of my own. Had I been content simply to enjoy their company, I might have realized that all things considered, they were doing fine."[6]

How we interpret what we see and hear affects us. Take the role of "memory tapes" in marital quarrels, for example. Instead of interpreting the present moment on the basis of present dynamics, spouses tend to interpret it on the basis of their memories of similar conflicts in the past. Since these memories are still charged with negative feelings, their projection at this time heats up the moment. For example, a wife corrected her husband's grammar when they were with his friends; her husband felt she was attacking his intelligence, because of his painful memories of such corrections in the past. Instead of being mildly annoyed at the public corrections, he was overwhelmed with violent feelings and withdrew into silence. His interpretation of what his wife interpreted as a helpful correction devastated his already shaky confidence about his intellectual abilities.

The situation is similar to that depicted by a *New York Magazine* cartoon entitled, *"Nanook Goes South."* The first picture shows Nanook in the cold north wearing his heavy parka. The second picture shows him in the same outfit in the hot south. He is "boiling in his parka," says the caption, "but old habits die hard." Memory tapes are like Nanook's parka. They are as irrelevant to the present moment as the parka was to Nanook's travel to the south. No wonder they generate heat!

Dated interpretations perpetuate game playing rather than congruent communication in our personal relationships. A daughter was frustrated with her elderly mother because her mother was always looking on the dark side of things, and all the daughter's attempts to help her see the positive side seemed only to entrench the mother more deeply in the negative. The daughter's interpretation, based largely on her own anxieties, was that her mother was on the verge of despondency and needed her daughter to pull her back from the brink.

With the help of a counselor, the daughter considered a different interpretation, namely, that the mother felt safe in being negative around the daughter because the daughter would always take the responsibility for being positive. With this different interpretation, the daughter tried a different approach. She concurred with her mother that things were really bad, and empathized rather than argued with her. The mother was confused by this change. Alarmed by the fact that her daughter was no longer the guarantor of the positive, she herself became positive. "Well," she admitted, "things are not all that bad, I guess. They could be worse—even a lot worse."

With no one else to reenforce the hidden positive within her, she had to do it herself. No longer able to play the game "Cheer me up while I frustrate your attempts," she herself was freed up to interpret her situation differently.

FAITH'S QUALITATIVE DIFFERENCE

How we interpret the present moment—its meaning and significance—is directly related to how we respond to it. Our religious faith can have everything to do with this response. A response of stress indicates that we perceive in the present situation a potentially overpowering threat. Religious faith not only provides a way of coping with this threat but also affects, by its own qualitative difference in perception, the way we interpret the threat.

This difference has been traditionally described as the "eye of faith," probably because of Jesus's words "Blessed are your eyes for they see" (Matt. 13:16). When we are under God, we see much more than our physical eyes alone can tell us. With the eye of faith, we see God hidden in the present moment, and this perception makes all the difference in the world in its effect on us.

When our awareness is narrow, we question few of our assumptions, so that we have fewer options. In so doing we "infinitize" the finite. When Einstein was asked how he became aware of the theory of relativity, he answered, "I challenged an axion."[7] Similarly, when theologian Karen Lebacqz addressed the Nobel Conference on Science at Gustavus Adolphus College, she said that religion's contribution to scientific inquiry is that it helps us question our assumptions. In other words, religion keeps the scientist from becoming dogmatic, because God alone is the ultimate; all other issues are penultimates. When we center ourselves in the ultimate through worship, we are shaken loose from our rigidities and arbitrary limitations, and this opens our perspective to other options.

Stress is caused not only by *what* happens to us but also by *how* we respond to it. We must here differentiate between external stress or *stressor*, and internal stress. External stresses are the problems and troubles we are experiencing—in our marriages, families, parishes or bodies. These stressors correspond to St. Paul's words "We are troubled on every side."

But internal stress is our *own* stressful response to these external stresses. While we may or may not be able to do anything about our external stresses, our internal stress is potentially within our control.

Precisely at this point—our internal response to external stress—our religious faith makes its initial contribution. From the view point of this "eye of faith," it makes sense to follow St. Paul and be not troubled by cares, have no anxiety, be not stressed. Instead, by prayer let our needs be made known unto God—the God hidden in this present moment of cares, whether these be cares over the parish, or over self-esteem, or over the family or peer or hierarchical tensions.

6. To Pray Is to Breathe

To deal religiously with stress, we turn to our source—our creator. "In everything by prayer and supplication with thanksgiving let your requests be made known unto God." Prayer is the clergy's own professional specialty.

Søren Kierkegaard compared prayer to breathing. It is an apt analogy for the choked feeling of stress. "The possibilities of prayer," he said, "are for the self what oxygen is for breathing."[1]

Henri Nouwen also sees prayer as a way of getting our breath: "There is probably no image that expresses so well the intimacy with God in prayer as the image of God's breath. We are the asthmatic people who are cured of their anxiety . . . we receive a new breath, a new freedom, a new life. . . . Prayer, therefore is God's breathing in us."[2]

When our lungs in both body and spirit are constricted by stress, prayer is a way of getting our breath because it opens to our perspective the possibilities of hope. When we pray, we enter the realm of the Spirit, which is not confined to the constriction created by stress. Prayer facilitates the leap of faith in the direction of God in whom these possibilities exist. "With God all things are possible" (Matt. 19:26). Kierkegaard sees in this idea of possibility the antidote to stress: "Possibility is the only saving remedy: given a possibility, and with that the desperate man breathes once more, he revives again; for without possibility a man cannot, as it were, draw breath."[3]

THE PRESENCE OF GOD IN THE PRESENT MOMENT

To get our breath we need to hope, and prayer helps us envision that hope. The apparently impenetrable boundaries that stress places on our perspective are penetrated by the eye of faith, and the functioning of this eye is nurtured by prayer. As we need to breathe with rhythmic constancy for the proper functioning of our bodies, so for the proper functioning of our persons we need to pray with similar constancy. "Pray constantly" is a New Testament prescription (1 Thess. 5:17). Since prayer is directed to God, praying constantly is really "practicing the Presence," to use seventeenth century spiritual counselor Brother Lawrence's classic description. Even as intimates are comfortably aware of each other's presence though no words are spoken, so constantly praying is more descriptive of this awareness of God's presence than of specific petitions being directed to him. At the same time, spoken communication is the mainstay for these nonverbal experiences of presence.

It may seem ironic that in the midst of church crises clergy should lose their consciousness of God's presence. Actually, however, being clergy in this context is really no different from being in any other occupation, even though the situation is more obviously religious. The stress that clergy feel, like the stress that others feel, can block one's awareness of God. What *we do* or what others are doing at these moments replaces our awareness that God also is *doing* something. In the midst of congregational tensions, believers sometimes become functional atheists.

We can face reality because we see beyond it—believing that God can work through and even use our traumas though he may not have willed them. Many things happen in this world—in congregations, at denominational headquarters, and in theological seminaries—and also in our lives, that are not necessarily God's will. Yet he is not powerless before these things; he can use them, detours though they may be. This capacity is his *Godness* in a fallen world. Being aware of this power makes a difference in how we interpret the happenings of the present moment.

For example, a man whom I was counseling had resigned

himself to his problem. Had it not been disrupting his marriage, he probably would not have come to see me. "It's the way I am," he said. "I've just assumed that nothing can be done about it." But although the personality orientation to which he was referring is difficult to change, his assumption that it couldn't be changed was probably the major obstacle to change.

Knowing that he was open to a religious approach, I said, "There's a big difference between saying something is *difficult* and saying it is *impossible.* Suppose I said, 'With God all things are possible.' What does this notion mean to you?" After reflecting a moment he said, "I hadn't thought of that before. I suppose it would mean that it is possible." Now the main question for him is—does he *want* it to be possible—which means, does *he* want to change?

Because God can use even what he does not will, we can believe that he is "bigger" than our blunders, our failures, our obstacles, and even the conspiracies of others against us that we may fear. He is not just God, but *our* God, who has covenanted himself to us in our baptism. He is here, he is there, he is with us, he is for us. This is why we offer our prayers *with thanksgiving*: "Let your requests be made known with thanksgiving." To have one like our God to turn to in our stresses is a reason to be thankful.

THE SEARCH FOR THE POSITIVE

Hans Selye says that to reduce stress we need to focus our thought on something positive. Thanksgiving is the religious answer to this need. The eye of faith provides us with a larger vision. The counterpart to Jesus's words, "Blessed are the eyes which see what you see" (Luke 12:23) is "Grateful are the seers for what they see." Gratitude is an expansive mind set, providing us with space for movement. It is the opposite mind set to bitterness that constricts and stifles. We are thankful not need *in* our troubles. Gratitude is a *eustress* and a vital ingredient in wellness.

C. Ward Crampton, noted gerontologist, lists five qualities of living needed for healthy aging, one which is praising God. We are always recipients when we are seeing with the eye of faith. It is possible, then, in such consistent seeing to develop gratitude as a state of being. Praising God—or praying with thanksgiving—is a healthy activity not only for the aged but also for the middle aged and for the young, because it expands rather than constricts our space.

There is a difference between praising God because of what we are receiving in our expanded vision, and praising him to fulfill an image of what a religious person is supposed to do. Some of us have conditioned ourselves to say "Praise the Lord" in every negative as well as positive situation as a way of counteracting our doubts, resentments, and fears. In so doing we are using our religion to avoid facing the negative rather than as a way of facing it positively. This avoidance is expressed in a compulsive praising of God that keeps the lid on one's inner demons rather than in a spontaneous praising God for his help in dealing with these demons. The positive attitude implied in praying with thanksgiving comes from taking a good hard look at evil within us and outside of us. We can be sustained in this look by the assurance that God is the ultimate victor even over evil.

There is also another way of focusing on the positive that, while not the same as that of the compulsive deniers, is still similar in its avoidance of the negative. I am referring to approaches typified by television preacher Robert Schuller's "possibility thinking" and Norman Vincent Peale's "power of positive thinking." Such approaches are based on a simplistic notion that if we focus on the positive, the negative will atrophy for lack of attention. True, staring at the negative only increases its negative hold on us. Also, no power for good is offered by *negative* thinking or *impossibility* thinking. And some people have been helped by these approaches to break loose from their negative fixations.

Still, focusing primarily if not entirely on the positive produces an illusionary perception of the world in which we live. A good example of this effect is a television Hour of Power sermon by Schuller entitled "Blessings Always Boomerang." "It is impossible for blessings not to boomerang," says Schuller. "Throw out smiles and smiles will come your way. Be friendly and you will be surrounded by friends. Be generous and life will be generous to you."⁴

Although Schuller acknowledges exceptions to this boomerang principle ("There are times when you throw out a smile and you receive a rebuff"), he warns against building a personal philosophy on the exceptions. And so would I. Yet when you experience such exceptions in any major way, they are not simply abstract, but concrete and total. For example, you can feel wiped out by betrayal and indifference. After three years of investing himself in Judas, Jesus was betrayed by him. It would hardly be a comfort to think of Judas as an exception, especially when this exception led Jesus to the cross. Such preaching offers no empathic identification with the blows and devastations that existentially mock any rational order to the universe, such as the "boomerang principle." I personally have felt alienated from religious people who insisted on being positive when I was suffering from the exceptional tragedy.

Sometimes evil does *not* atrophy when attention is not paid to it; in fact, it may become entrenched by such avoidance. It is not coincidental that possibility thinkers tend to be conservative thinkers in their sociopolitical and economic views. The prophetic exposure of injustice and oppression in the social order (of which we are part) obviously upsets a positive focus. So some people feel they must mitigate, rationalize, or even evade any concern about these evils. Although generous in gifts to *have-nots*, simplisticly positive people tend to support control by the *haves*. Clergy are particularly susceptible to this temptation because, being influential in the community, they tend to be rewarded by powerful people for any support of the status quo—from which they also profit.

The positive focus that relieves stress is not that of the compulsive or philosophical minimizer of the negative, but rather that of a courageous confronter of the negative, who with the eye of faith, sees in, with, and under these evils the hidden presence of God. Before we can let go of the negative, we must take hold of it. The *resurrection* takes place after the *crucifixion*. People who want to let go without taking hold want to be resurrected without experiencing the cross.

In like manner, if we are to help others in trouble, we first need to identify with them in their trouble—to feel their pain— to have compassion. "The beginning of healing is in the solidarity with the pain."[5] Compassion, or empathy, with the negative feelings and experiences of others is the bridge over which the positive we have to offer is received. Jesus's healing of others occurred as he was moved with compassion for them (Mark 1:41). We cannot be a positive influence on one another if we do not first identify with one other's negative thinking.

At the same time, we may *overidentify* to the point where we lose contact—eye of faith contact—with the positive. Then, instead of one, two people need help—a not uncommon pitfall for clergy who are heavily involved in the pains of others.

By the same token, we sometimes take hold of our own negative feelings and realities and then, instead of letting them go, continue to hold on to them. A specific example is our tendency in stress to see only what is stressing us rather than to focus also on God, who can help us deal with these stresses. In fact, we assume that this concentration on our distress is helpful; worrying is often looked on as a way of working on the problem. Selye however, compares worry, as a "mental overreaction," with the tendency of our pro-inflammatory hormones to produce the overreactions known as *allergies*. In the case of hayfever, for example, the pollen is really a harmless invader; the pro-inflammatory overreaction is what is harmful.

It overestimates the problem and not only worsens the problem by overreacting but actually helps create it. And so, in a similar way, does worry create problems.[6]

At this point, I need to distinguish *worry* from *apprehension*. As I indicated previously, apprehension, though mildly stressful, moves one to anticipate reality. Apprehension can lead to preparatory action because it perceives where this action needs to be taken. But worry is really stress for stress's sake. Worry satisfies a need to be uncomfortable because being comfortable doesn't fit with one's self-image. At the same time, one feels more in control if one is worrying (that is, *doing* something) and less in control if one's attention is elsewhere (that is, "neglecting" the problem).

Actually, worrying only increases the stress. The more attention we give to anxiety, the more it tends to increase and consume us, because anxiety feeds on attention. Yet this very anxiety seduces us into thinking that if we focus on it we can resolve it. We become possessed by it, and instead of staying in control, we lose all control. This syndrome is another example of the need to be *as* God, in control. If, however, we feel ourselves to be *under* God, we can trust in the *higher* control.

WALKING ON WATER

The story of Peter's attempt to walk on water illustrates the loss of control that comes from focusing only on what is distressing us. Jesus sent his disciples by boat to the other side of the sea, which was choppy because of high winds. After a time the disciples believed they saw Jesus coming toward them walking on the water. Was it an apparition? Impulsive by nature, Peter tried to find out. "Lord, if it is you, bid me come to you on the water." Jesus told him to come. Peter got out of the boat to do so. Then the Gospel writer says, "But when he saw the wind, he was afraid and beginning to sink he cried out, 'Lord, save me' " (Matt. 14:22–23).

The implication is that had Peter kept his eyes on Jesus the story might have been different. But Peter deserves credit for knowing what to do when he *was* sinking—he cried out for help: "Lord, save me." Jesus immediately reached out his hand and caught him.

Martial arts provide an analogy to this story. I had a brief exposure to martial arts in a human potential workshop. After pairing us off, our instructor told one of each pair to imagine a garden hose coming from the abdomen and extending out on the lower side of one's arm, which was extended toward the opposite wall. We "defenders" were then to "see" the water from the hose hitting this wall. Our partners (the "attackers") were told to take our extended arm and throw us off balance. We were to prevent this attack by keeping our eyes fixed on the wall where the "water" was hitting as it came from our "hose." To everyone's amazement, our partners found it difficult and in some cases impossible to pull us off balance.

Then we were told to take our eyes off the wall where the "water" was hitting and to look instead at the fingers of the extended arm. Our partners were again instructed to pull us off balance, and we were to resist. This time our partners had an easy time. When we projected our mental visualization beyond ourselves, our bodies became centered and in some cases immovable. We could not be pulled off balance, as one might expect in this vulnerable position. But when we focused our eyes and minds on our own fingers, we were easily thrown off balance.

In like manner, our most stress-free position is when we take our eyes off what is distressing us—not out of fear of looking at it, because we *have* looked at it—and look instead to Jesus in response to his invitation, "Come to me all who labor and are heavy laden, and I will give you rest" (Matt. 11:28). In this position we are stabilized, and it is difficult for us to be thrown off balance. In this position, Jesus said, we "learn from him" (Matt. 11:29). Because we are looking in his direction, we are positioning ourselves "under God." This stabilization process is described biblically as "establishing our hearts" (1 Thess. 3:13, James 5:8). Both the Greek word that we translate as *establish*, and the Latin word from which the word *establish* comes, mean "to make stable, firm, to be centered."

In this position we are balanced, with our center beyond as well as within us. This is where the center needs to be if we are created in God's image. According to this biblical psychology, we humans are created for relationship. The essence of our being is in communion with our creator. The "fall" disrupted this communion. God's redemption in Christ from the fall restored us to this communion. Our humanity has a transcendent dimension, which is traditionally described as our "spirit." When our spirit is in dialogue with God's Spirit we are centered, stable, the way we were meant to be, fully human.

THE LIBERATION OF OUR SPIRIT

Sometimes we can't do much about what is stressing us, and those with whom we have sought counsel may be just as unable, because the external stress is beyond our control. I was counseling with a woman who was in this situation, and so was I. Her problems were severe, but their resolution depended in part on the cooperation of others (in this case, family members), and this cooperation was not forthcoming. What could I do for her? What could she do for herself?

I helped her to return to the practice of prayer, which in her discouragement she had dropped, and she learned over a period of time to live with her problems in a positive way. The trouble was the same, but *she* wasn't. Her own words were "It's like I'm back to my center—I'm not panicky, unglued, unbalanced anymore." Her problems had "thrown" her off center and off balance. Through prayer, she got straight once again concerning who God is; therefore she knew again who she was—a child of God—and her balance was restored.

Her experience paralleled that of Job, whose onslaught of troubles disrupted his perspective of life and of God, and of how God operates. He couldn't understand why such awful things were allowed to happen to him, or as Rabbi Harold Kushner puts it, why "bad things happen to good people." As we know, Job didn't break off communion with God. Rather, he continued to quarrel with him, sometimes demanding, sometimes pleading, for an answer. With the help of Elihu, his fourth pastoral caregiver, he finally heard God speak to him. After this experience, his perspective changed. Before any of his troubles were relieved, Job came to peace with them. He was centered, stabilized, under God. Or as Job says, "I had heard of thee by the hearing of the ear but now my eye sees thee" (Job 42:5).

As Elihu saw it, Job had received "songs in the night" (35:10)—inner peace in external stress. We can live positively with unanswered questions and unresolved problems when our center is in our dialogue with God, because then we can trust.

For our purpose Augustine's familiar words, "Our souls are restless, O Lord, until they find their rest in thee," can be paraphrased as "Our souls are stressful, O Lord, until they find their ease in thee." The basic liberation occurs when we are liberated from the compulsion to be as God. This change is basic because it liberates our spirit. It does not liberate us from our external stress but from our bondage to it. It is the equivalent of salvation. We are set free from the destructive influence of stress, and free to enter into our human identity wherein lies our health, our wellness.

7. Achieving Balance in the Life of the Ministry

When we take a balanced perspective—in how we interpret what we see and hear and what happens to us—we have a natural resistance to stress and stress-related illnesses. Achieving this balanced perspective now and then is one thing; sustaining and reenforcing it is another. The best way I know to do this latter is to live a balanced life.

CULTURAL RESISTANCE TO BALANCE IN LIVING

Our cultural values and priorities, however, make it difficult to achieve this balance. In a stress workshop for clergy, one of the pastors related the putdown he had received when he asked the cooperation of his council to achieve a better balance in his living. "I explained to them that I was working too much and beginning to get some physical symptom warnings, so I was planning to cut back to a more manageable load. After a moment or so of silence, the chairman cleared his throat and said, 'Well, pastor, the way I operate in my business is that if the work's there, it's got to be done.' "

In a recent visit to Australia visiting church conferences, it was evident to me (and I was also informed by the Australian people with whom I visited) that despite the similarities of our peoples and languages, Australians lack that drive and pressure to produce and achieve that characterizes the United States. An interesting reflection of this difference is the practice of the Lutheran Church of Australia to give all its clergy the same salary. Whether they are veterans or beginners, pastors of large or small churches, the president of the seminary or the lowly instructor, they each receive the same remuneration, with small additions for each child. Lutherans in the United States and most other denominations here subscribe to a (stressful) differentiated salary structure for their clergy similar to the economic market place.

Under this pressure of our cultural values and priorities, people can consume almost all their time and energy in their jobs and/or family responsibilities, and this depletion lowers their resistance to stress. Some, of course, neglect their family responsibilities for their jobs. Most such workers are men. As a counselor, I have been impressed over and again by some men's assumption that their job demands have priority over everything else. And although their wives do not like the effect on family living, they usually do not question such assumptions. Clergy*men* tend to have these same assumptions about their work as other men in our culture, but they feel more guilt over it because they realize from their pastoral education that they have responsibilities also for their marriage and family. Their wives feel similarly to other wives about their deprivation, but they tend to have a more available scapegoat for their resentment, namely, the congregation.

Some people—mostly women—also neglect a balance in living because of family responsibilities. Some of this neglect is caused by the need to take up slack left by the men. Moreover, in his therapy with the Brown family, for example, family therapist Salvador Minuchin shows how the interlocking family system functions to bolster Mrs. Brown's overinvestment in her children:

The mother will not let her children go until the father offers her support and tenderness as a husband. As long as contact between the father and children takes place only via the mother, the father and mother cannot move in their own spouse orbit. While the mother and father remain divided, the children must continue to struggle with the mother's intrusive overnurturance and overcontrol.[1]

Yet not all of some women's overinvestment in their children is due to intrafamily dynamics. Cultural pressures also bear on women in regard to their motherhood. We tend to assume that the primary responsibility for rearing children belongs to the woman. Consequently, measurement of the woman's worth in this instance is tied up with how she functions as a mother.

The result of these pressures on both men and women is that we tend to invest too many ego needs into work and/or family. Single parents (whose number is rapidly increasing and who are usually women), bear a double pressure at this point.

People seem more likely to seek a balance in living when the imbalance is caused by economic necessity or even physical survival than when it is caused by ego overinvestment. My grandfather, for example, worked as a puddler in the sweltering heat of a steel mill twelve hours a day, six days a week, with no paid vacations. Yet every July the steel mill workers would strike—and be off work for six to eight weeks before reaching a settlement. It made survival sense, even though they received no remuneration from their union, to take the summer off, through the only way open to them—a strike, although it was hard economically on the family.

It makes just as much sense to take this risk for balance when our imbalance comes from the pressure to prove ourselves in our responsibilities, but we feel less free then to take such a risk. Being judged as a failure in our culture is evidently a greater threat than being deprived in our physical needs. And although the church holds to a different value system, clergy seem to feel a similar compulsion regarding their work.

The way to restore balance to our lives is to develop activities other than work and family responsibilities. These other interests and activities in turn help to keep work and family responsibilities from becoming *too* important. When work becomes habitually all consuming, we lose our flexibility because of our heavy ego investment. We tend to be more effective in both job and family living when we project fewer ego needs into them.

TIME FOR SPIRITUAL DEVELOPMENT

Time for other interests and activities means first of all time for spiritual development, specifically time for prayer and meditation. As a seminary student, I heard my professor quote Martin Luther's familiar words that he had so much to do on a particular day that he had to get up earlier to have even more time for prayer. I heard this statement as a pious attitude toward prayer but hardly one that I—or my professors—would really put into practice. Now, however, I hear it differently. Besides being pious, Luther was also being sensible. In facing a particularly demanding day, he knew he needed to take the time to get himself centered, focused, under God, so he would be sensitive to the needs of others and open to the Spirit's guidance.

In our culture taking extra time for prayer on a particularly busy day would seem only to add to the stress, because it would just be one more thing to be done! When work is religious in nature, it might seem logical to cut short our prayers in order to get at all the work that God wants done. But prayer, particularly when associated with meditation, is actually not an activity to be *done* as much as a *ceasing* from doing. At least it is a different kind of activity from that which we usually associate with getting things done. Meditation is a way of listening to the Spirit, of observing God's hand in our life, of slowing the frenetic pace of our minds, of being still in the presence of God, of focusing total attention on his Word. It is a time of centering, of focusing on God, of getting our identity straight as creatures under the creator. When we get off center, our focus becomes fuzzy. Luther was wise—it saves time on busy days first to get centered so that we know who is God. From this position of centering, we offer prayers of petition and intercession, committing the tension areas of life to God, in the quietness and trust that is our strength (Is. 30:15).

TIME FOR HOBBIES

Time for other interests also includes hobbies. A hobby is only a hobby when it is a distraction from work. People who plan to spend their time on their hobbies when they retire or when hit by unemployment, usually find that in actuality they don't. Hobbies tend to lose their attraction when they become the main pursuit. But when used to balance work, a hobby helps us keep our perspective on work from becoming distorted. We are then also easier to work *with*. Our minds need other mental challenges than those associated with work. We need a minivacation during the day for a change of stimulation. This change in focus also helps us to keep our identity under God, because we have to put aside other responsibilities—in a sense, committing them to God—while we focus on something the purpose of which is enjoyment.

My hobby is gardening, particularly flower gardening. I like to see plants grow, just as I like to see people grow. In the summer I like to get up in the morning to see how each plant looks because then they are at their best. But I have a hard time keeping this pursuit as a hobby. I would say to myself, "I'm going to spend an hour in the garden." But at the end of the hour I would see one more thing that needed doing—and another—until one hour became two, and I was just as unwilling to quit then as before. My completion compulsion was threatening to take the joy out of my gardening. Ironically, my hobby was becoming a source of stress.

I had already given up golf for this same reason—I felt worse after playing than before. But I didn't want to give up gardening, because I like it. So I had to face up to a reality: just as God accepts the incomplete, so can I. If God can accept me in my inadequacy, who am I not to be able to accept my inadequate garden?

It was a liberating realization. I have accepted—with some unevenness—my incomplete, inadequate, bug-ridden, weed-infested garden, and I enjoy it. Most of the time I know when to quit. The revelation saved my hobby.

TIME FOR PHYSICAL EXERCISE

A balanced life includes time for the body, especially for physical exercise. The Biblical understanding of us humans is that the person is interrelated with the body. True, the Greek world dominated by Platonic thought viewed the body as a hindrance to the spirit. And the Platonic Greek world has heavily influenced the Western, traditional understanding of Christianity. However, the doctrine of creation in the Judeo-Christian tradition affirms the body as a fit expression for the spirit. Taking care of our bodies, thus, is really taking care of *ourselves*.

Just as the spirit needs exercise in prayer and meditation, so also the body needs exercise to stimulate the cardiovascular and muscular systems. Without such exercise, we grow weak. For example, as women grow older they tend to develop osteoporosis—their bones become brittle and break. This condition can be prevented by exercise, among other measures, such as increasing the intake of calcium and vitamin D. Also our need to give rides to people, particularly the elderly, to their very doors, except for safety purposes, implies that walking must be bad for them. Exactly the opposite is true. We would be doing them and ourselves more of a favor by walking with them.

Moreover, walking with people provides an excellent setting for pastoral visitation. I learned this approach while a graduate student at Boston University School of Theology. If a student desired a conference with the revered professor Edgar Sheffield Brightman, Brightman invited the student to join him for a walk. I don't recall ever visiting him that we were not walking somewhere, and after nearly forty years I can still remember the content of those visits.

Running, swimming, biking, and even brisk walking also help reduce stress. It is a positive sign that so many people today are doing these activities. My wife and I take a hiking trip each summer as a conditioner for the Minnesota winter.

Last summer, hiking in St. Croix State Park in Minnesota, we met a caretaker on the trail who told us that he has to maintain the paths much more carefully than in the past because so many more people are using them.

But television's influence for the sedentary life is still strong. Pittsburgh Steeler quarterback Terry Bradshaw hit the nail on the head when he said, "Football is a game in which 22 big, strong, healthy guys run around like crazy for two hours while 50,000 people, who really need the exercise, watch them." And, we might add, "the 50,000,000 watching them on television."

When lamenting the addictive effect of television, we usually think of the children who watch television six to seven hours a day, or of the women and the elderly who are addicted to the soap operas. But we rarely mention the men who are addicted to televised sports. These men believe (in a subliminal way) that they have had a physical workout in their intense involvement in watching the televised game. Yet this workout is as illusionary as is the fantasy relationships that others develop in their addiction to the characters in television dramas. Such dramas' relevance to real personal lives is as realistic as thinking that the action in the game is *their* action in spite of their sedentary position.

The British stress researcher, Malcolm Carruthers, tested spectators at football games and discovered that they showed the excitement of the players—pulse rate up 40 percent and extra fats and sugars released into the bloodstream—but that this buildup was not expended by physical activity as it was by the players. Carruthers also tested people working out in a gymnasium and found that people who exercise regularly can do three to six times as much work for a given pulse rate, sharply reduce their levels of cholesterol, and not only act less fatigued but are easier to get along with.[2]

People who exercise regularly often comment about how good they feel. Researchers believe that when our bodies are highly stimulated through exercise they produce their own endorphins, chemicals similar to morphine that are produced in the brain and pituitary gland. Researchers from Massachusetts General Hospital measured endorphin levels in volunteers and found that their levels of endorphin rose with regular exercise. Taking blood samples before and after exercising, the researchers discovered that after two months of workouts the subjects' endorphin levels were up 145 percent following an hour of exercise. Endorphins evidently block pain signals to the brain and stimulate the parts of the brain associated with good feelings—elation and pleasure.[3]

Obviously, we were not created to be sedentary, a condition that predisposes us to disease. The automobile and other labor-saving technological achievements have made us more efficient time-wise but have also undermined our health and perhaps even our life spans. So they may not have saved us that much time. Even people confined to wheelchairs are finding it beneficial to participate in various games and contests that bring as much physical stimulation to their bodies as possible under the circumstances.

TIME FOR SOCIAL DEVELOPMENT

Time for other activities includes times for social development, which St. Paul called "practicing hospitality" (Rom. 12:13). We need to cultivate our friendships, relating intimately to real people. As an old proverb says, "A shared joy is double joy; a shared sorrow is half sorrow."

Social development is not the same as socializing. Many social gatherings, in fact, can leave us feeling more lonely than before. Phyllis McGinley, with her light touch of humor, reflects on the superficiality of such events in her poem "Reflections at Dawn":

> Oh! there is many a likely boon
>   That fate might flip me from her griddle.
> I wish that I could sleep till noon
>   And play the fiddle,
> Or dance a *tour jete* so light

It would not shake a single straw down.
But when I ponder how last night
  I laid the law down,
More than to have the Midas touch
  Or critic's praise, however hearty,
I wish I didn't talk so much
I wish I didn't talk so much
I wish I didn't talk so much
  When I am at a party.[4]

We need friendships in which we can enjoy the other's presence and feel comfortable in it. An acquaintance is one thing, a friend is another. With friends we feel accepted and receive the support we need in our stressful environment. Not everybody is even potentially a friend, however. A certain attraction of "chemistry" is needed. But the potential may also be present and not developed. For social development, we need to take the initiative and be sufficiently secure in our own identity to reach out to those with whom we would like to be friends. Not everybody will respond, and not all initial attractions prove durable, but in the long run initiatives for friendship produce their good effects.

Both as individuals and in their marriages, clergy have a difficult time forming mutual friendships with other people and couples. Developing friendships with people for whom one is also pastor is complicated by this additional responsibility. Therefore the usual concerns are valid about choosing intimate friends who are also parishioners. Friendships that do not have this complexity of roles are obviously "safer." Yet the pastor may not always have this option, particularly in more isolated areas. Also, both clergy and spouse may feel drawn to specific members. If the choice is between having intimate friends within the congregation or not having them at all, then having them within the congregation is the better choice. Pastors and their spouses, like anybody else, function better as people and as mates when they have both personal and couple friends beyond their marriage.

A FOUR POINT PROGRAM

I use the concept of the balanced life as resource in my pastoral counseling because it provides people with concrete goals toward which they can work in helping themselves. Pastor Ann, for example, was motivated to work toward these goals largely to get over her depression. Although depression is a subject in itself, it is also a form of stress. Ann had been depressed before and had come out of it through the use of antidepressant drugs. This time she wanted to help herself without drugs.

I asked her if she was willing to invest her time and energy in ways that would counteract her depression. I suggested the following holistic emphases of a balanced life:

1. Spend twenty minutes in the morning and evening in prayer and meditation.
2. Develop a program of regular physical exercise.
3. Take the initiative to have a social engagement twice a week.
4. Due to the frequent interaction of physiological as well as spiritual factors in depression, eat only nutritious food, such as fruits and vegetables, avoiding foods made with processed sugar and white flour, including soft drinks; and eat fish and poultry along with red meat.

Ann protested a bit. Each of these directives would be difficult for her. Acknowledging the difficulty, I reminded her that since she wanted to overcome her depression without resorting to medication, this program was one way of attempting to do so. She accepted the challenge and committed herself to these goals. We then used the counseling sessions to look into the painful areas in her life that were feeding her depression.

Ann succeeded in overcoming depression without medication. I had anticipated this success; what impressed me was how much less counseling time it took than I expected. Each activity that I gave Ann to do was itself an anti-depressant.

She herelf was therefore doing most of what needed to be done.

Moreover, when she was feeling better, Ann felt no need to curtail her involvement in a balanced life, as she would have with medication. "I like running," she said. "In fact, I've learned to do my meditating while I run. I like them both better that way. Good food soon tastes good or better than the soft drinks and sweet rolls, and I enjoy getting together with friends." The balanced life—beside being a resource in holistic counseling—is the ounce of prevention that is worth the pound of cure.

ORGANIZED EFFECIENCY

When our lives are balanced, we are more efficient in our work. Stress makes us inefficient; it is like having an inner friction that must be overcome, so our efforts take more energy than is really necessary for the job itself. A balanced life, however, not only relieves stress but also protects leisure. By providing a needed contrast to busyness, leisure thus contributes to work efficiency.

In the church to which I belong, the retired seniors' group is called the Leisure Club. The implication is obvious that leisure comes when our working days are over. Yet even as older people need to continue to work for a balanced life, so working people also need to protect their leisure for their own effectiveness. We miss something very vital to our humanity when we have no time and energy for leisure. Then we don't have the opportunity to "smell the flowers," as Watergate conspirator John Dean said in describing what led to his downfall. Without leisure in our lives, our perspective can become distorted, and our sense of values become confused.

When we balance our lives, we become better organized. In organizing ourselves, we are expressing our freedom, because we determine our own priorities and decide how we want to live, how to spend out time. Instead of being driven to conform to external pressures, we can direct ourselves; that is, we can make our own decisions and be sufficiently integrated to carry them out. This spiritual discipline enables us to respond to God's call, and in so doing to take charge of our own lives. The word *organize* has a late Latin root word meaning to play an organ. To play an organ one must get all 1,500 pipes to sound in harmony. Moreover, a balanced perception is not simply a mind set, but a response to God's call. When we are under God, we are called by God. He calls us into harmony with his Spirit and therefore with our own humanity. This calling or commitment is like the musical score that puts the sounds of the organ's many pipes into a harmonious whole. It *organizes* us. Our meaning and purpose lie beyond ourselves. They center in our transcendence in which our spirit reaches out to the Spirit of God in the communion for which we were created. We stay on top of things better when we stay under God.

Finally, when clergy take charge of themselves and live a balanced life as much as possible amid the emergencies of ministry, they are at the same time modeling this life for the people to whom they minister. Because stress is such a universal problem in our culture, the ministry of modeling is a powerful backup for other ministries in helping people cope positively with this "killer." And clergy and their families are the first to profit personally from such modeling.

8. Getting Control of Our Lives

In order to achieve personal organization, which puts all the parts of our lives into a harmonious whole, we need to exercise the freedom we have under God to take control of our lives. As long as we are reacting in a knee-jerking fashion to pressures from within or from without, we remain in bondage. So whether the stimulus triggers the predictable emotions of anger, fear, panic, and guilt—or the equally predictable attitudes of resentment, retaliation, or defensiveness—such a reaction precludes any freedom to *choose* a response. Obviously we are out of control, and we even refer to this condition in precisely these words. So wherein lies our hope to change these predictable patterns?

The first step toward this change is to decide whether we want to continue in such stimulus-reaction bondage. If we decide we do not, we have taken the first step. The next step is to face up to our double-mindedness, our ambivalence. We need to recognize that we are not only in bondage to our reactions, but we are also to some extent *affirming* these reactions. We are getting some satisfaction from them, however perverse, that perpetuates the bondage. We have the freedom to give up these satisfactions. When we can put a single, undivided mind behind the desire to change, we have released the resources God has given us for change. The third step is to believe that this decision is not just our decision but also God's, and to hear and to see him calling us to move in this direction.

Eric Berne's term *permission* touched a responsive chord in our society. People seemed to be longing for permission that would free them to act. The biblical resource for this freedom includes permission but goes beyond it. The word is *calling*. A permission giver may not care whether or not one takes advantage of the permission. But when God calls us, God cares about our response. God *wants* us free, healthy, and fulfilled.

Believing that God is calling us is the strongest motivation to move out of our destructive ways, to overcome our habitual inertia, to challenge our low expectations. Unfortunately, some stress researchers, including Selye, understand this religious influence for motivation as a response to a command. To them, religion is *law*. But *calling*, in differentiation from command, is Gospel, or good news. It is the embrace and vision of love.

To reach the clarity of mind implied by responding to a divine calling, most of us need to deal with our resistance to what we supposedly want. This double-mindedness eats away at us, generating stress and leading ultimately to burnout. The stress of burnout is often connected with being inwardly resistant to at least some of the activities of being a parish pastor. This source of stress is best dealt with by cultivating openness in our relationships and by acknowledging how we feel—to ourselves, to God, and to significant others. As we share what is going on within us, we ourselves learn what it is. Then we are in a position to make intelligent decisions in regard to our needs.

We surrender much of our control over our lives because we are afraid to deal directly with interpersonal conflict. To avoid this conflict, we deny or at least minimize a lot of reality. The *will* to be ignorant has kept many of us ignorant. In a fearful attempt to limit our awareness, we don't ask the questions we *could* ask. This "sweeping under the rug" of what we don't want to face forfeits our control because in effect we are thereby deciding not to be responsible.

Actually, what we don't know *can* hurt us, and badly. The belief that what we do not face will go away, sooner or later will be exposed as an illusion. In the meantime, much valuable time and opportunity has been lost. This attitude is like refusing to recognize disease symptoms out of fear that one might have the disease, until the debilitating effects can no longer be denied—and then discovering that the disease, like most problems, has a more hopeful prognosis when treated early.

Much strain on the job and in our families manifests itself in strained relationships. For example, many of us don't talk directly to the people with whom we are in conflict. This direct talking is the hardest thing to do, so we don't do it. Instead we minimize the problem, or we talk critically *about* the people with whom we are in conflict, or we let out our irritations toward them in indirect ways that are destructive.

At such times we need to ask ourselves, "What seems threatening about dealing openly with conflict? What are we afraid might happen? Are we afraid that our egos will be bruised in the ensuing exchange, or that we will replay old tapes that we would like to think no longer exist?

Since we are brought up in our culture to believe that the best defense is a good offense, many of us begin with a display of anger. Andrew Jackson was known, for example, for his violent verbal attacks on others. Yet according to historian Arthur M. Schlesinger, Jr., Jackson deliberatedly feigned his anger: "His towering rages were actually his way of avoiding futile argument." Rather than being trapped in stimulus-reaction bondage, he *chose* to appear furious to intimidate his critics. When they left in haste, he would coolly light his pipe and chuckle over the fact that they thought he was angry.[1]

We not only fear other people's anger but also our own impulses. We may feel that if we dealt directly with conflict and stirred up not only the other person's anger but also our own, we ourselves might slip out of control. The fear of anger, then, can be a fear of our own inner chaos. As is often the case, however, the fear of something happening is often worse than the reality. When we overcome our fear of anger in order to improve our relationships, we usually discover that we have become more capable of taking charge of our anger.

A CULTURE HUNG UP ON ANGER

In the United States, we find it hard to cope with anger in our culture. But we are a most violent people with a frightening murder rate per capita compared to other nations. Such rage stems from our repression of anger. And difficulties with anger create much of our stress.

Clergy are just as troubled by anger as are lay people. Those same people (both clergy and laity) who wear smiles to church can be notorious for angry exchanges at council and particularly at congregational meetings. Clergy, however, are not supposed to have anger, let alone display it. "I was playing golf with a foursome from the congregation," said one pastor, "and I messed up a strategic shot. I got mad, and the others noticed. 'I didn't think pastors would get angry like that,' said one." But why would it be unexpected for pastors to be angry unless there is also a judgment on anger in itself?

Precisely this judgment complicates the management of anger. In guilt, some people repress their anger, letting it eat away at their stomach lining. Others also attempt to control anger by holding it in, but eventually the pressure is too great and the held-back anger explodes, rupturing relationships. Others flare impulsively, sending their blood pressure sky high. They "lose their temper" which means they become rigid like untempered steel, and break reather than bend. Their blood vessels may bear the brunt.

For this discussion of clergy stress, however, the most important issues regarding anger is that it prevents us from carrying out our best insights. Unresolved anger jaundices our perspective, particularly toward certain people or issues. Moreover, it comes out indirectly, seeping out sideways, even when we try to "put our best foot forward." And other people sense our anger even when we are not consciously communicating it.

ANGER IN OTHER STRESSES

Anger is involved in most of our stresses. For example, frustration is a reaction to being blocked from doing what we want to do, such as when our plans and hopes for the congregation are thwarted. We relive the rage of an infant who is physically restrained from moving, in such restraints on our desires. Moreover, when we are blocked, we are more than enraged—we are also frightened, because whatever takes away our control frightens us. In order to replicate human stress in rats as closely as possible, Selye hobbled them with cotton shackles so that they were severely restrained in their movements. Their frustration created severe stress. "A rat wants to have his own way," comments Selye, "just like a human being, and does not like to be prevented from doing what he wants to do."[2]

Some people express their frustration in forbidden profanity. This symbol of rebellion may give the sensation of throwing off restraints. Because these words have a long association with frustration, however, their use may actually accelerate one's sense of frustration and discomfort.

The stress of irritation is also based on anger. Working with people, like living with them, exposes us to all sorts of annoyances. Some overcritical people are forever badgering us about something, and some people continually play on one string and play it once too often. Then irritation sends an unpleasant sensation "zinging" through our brain and then into our gut.

Irritation accumulates easily because those who annoy us usually are not attacking us directly. So we rarely deal with annoyance at the moment. Nonetheless, the annoyances still register on our consciousness, often belatedly. After churning about within us for a while, the irritation may subside, only to be aroused again in the next incident when the irritation may be even more intense, inwardly "tying us in knots."

Anger is a major component in the stress of disappointment.

In fact, therapist Albert Ellis maintains that anger is essentially disappointment and that we ought to say we are disappointed with someone rather than angry with him or her. We feel let down in our disapointments, particularly when we had high anticipations. We feel hurt because certain people have not taken us seriously, or have even exploited us. And when projects to which we have devoted much time and energy do not work out, we may feel personally defeated. The hoped-for achievement promised not only progress but also purpose, so the disappointment is shattering. And thus anger seems to give us at least a negative expression of freedom.

Anger is also involved in the widespread stress of depression. Although someone who is depressed looks anything but angry, anger is present in most depressions. When anger is too conscious or too large to repress, some of us turn it in on ourselves. When we see no acceptable outlet or target for our anger, we may find living with it as depression less threatening, perhaps because we believe it is less threatening to those about us.

Despite their phlegmatic appearance, people who are depressed are in inward stress, even agitation. Although depression may be a distorted way of coping with stress, it is also a symptom of the person's crumbling resistance to stress. In this latter sense it is comparable to the exhaustion stage of the General Adaptation Syndrome. If the irritation that brings about the body's General Adaptation Syndrome continues over a very long time, the affected cells eventually break down from fatigue. If the condition persists, the cells become exhausted and the body dies

TWO THERAPEUTIC APPROACHES TO ANGER

There are two major therapeutic approaches in dealing with anger. The first is the cathartic approach of therapists such as George Bach and Theodore Rubin, who feel that people should let out anger in a safe and constructive way. The second is the cognitive approach of therapists such as Albert Ellis and Aron

Beck, who believe that people should change their irrational assumptions or beliefs that generate anger. Ellis, like the Epistle of James, believes that the "anger of people does not work the righteousness of God" (James 1:20)—even though Ellis does not believe in God. Consequently, the more rational our assumptions, the less we need anger.

These two appraoches seem directly opposed to each other. Bach is saying, in effect, "Let out your feelings in a healthy way, and your thinking will straighten out"; Ellis is saying, "Straighten out your thinking, and your feelings will become positive." We can compare Bach's approach to that of the psalmists in the unrestrained expression of their anger, to Job's angry attacks on God, and to Paul's biting remarks regarding the Judaizers in the Epistle to the *Galatians*.

Ellis's approach requires us to question our assumptions. As previously indicated, this questioning is precisely what our religion helps us to do. By giving us a larger perspective within which to view the constraints of the moment, we are likely to feel less threatened than if confined to the "universe" of sensory perceptions and our own fragile existence. The irrational assumptions that generate anger are largely the product of a self-curved-in-on-itself (*incurvatus in se*) in which functionally at least we are behaving "as God."

Anger is a primary passion when it is a reaction against instances of human injustice and oppression. This is the prophetic anger against the exploitation and dehumanization of one people by another described in the Bible. Anger may also be a secondary passion in that it is a reaction to one's fear or guilt or hurt. The former is not reducable, being the proper reaction to human injustice. The latter, which is obviously reducable, is usually best dealt with at the level of the feelings that are stimulating it. Obviously we need to recognize what is generating anger in order to do this, and evaluating our assumptions is a good beginning.

Family therapist Virginia Satir has an intermediate position between Bach's cathartic appraoch and Ellis's cognitive approach.

Her approach focuses on the question "How do you *feel* about feeling angry?" How we interpret our feelings has much to do with their effect on us. If I feel soiled by my anger, for example, I am functioning on the assumption or belief that anger is bad. On what do I base this assumption? From whom or from what did I receive it? On what criteria do I evaluate it and ultimately retain or change it?

APPLYING THE APPROACH THAT IS NEEDED

Rather than being directly opposed to each other, the cathartic and cognitive approaches are complimentary. By itself, either one is unbalanced because it applies to specific individuals rather than to all people. Our individual hangups with anger determine which way is best for us.

Some of us are blamers, for example, and tend to justify our anger on the basis of the unfair or cruel actions of others. Satir describes the blamer as one whose sentences begin with, "You never do this, or you always do that, or why do you always, or why do you never . . . " The blamer, she says, is "much more interested in throwing his weight around than really finding out about anything."[3]

If we are blamers, we obviously need a wider perspective within which to interpret reality. Such outrage at the behavior of others is based on the assumption that they dare not do this (whatever) to us! Because we are already openly angry, expressing anger may not resolve it. Instead we may continue to generate anger because our assumption about our privileged position in the universe does not fit the kind of world in which we live. Jesus made it plain that we can anticipate criticism or unfair treatment because of the fallenness of the human condition. Why then should it be so outrageous that it should happen to you or to me? Even more important, why should it be such a blow to our egos?

The cognitive approach, thus, helps those of us who not only know we are angry but who also tend to justify it or even nurse it. Our assumptions or belief systems generate anger unnecessarily; other assumptions or beliefs more in line with reality could diffuse it.

Yet the cognitive appraoch might fortify the rationalizations of those of us who are reluctant to acknowledge or to admit to our anger. "What good does it do to deal with anger?" we might say as justification for not dealing with it.

If you tend to keep your anger to yourself so that it takes its toll on your mental and physical health, consider instead what Bach has to say about "letting it out." The cathartic approach adapts very well to a biblical model. In a prayerful awareness of the presence of God, we can face up to our feelings. Then we will realize who it is or what it is that angers us. Like the psalmist, we can let go of our anger toward this person or that situation. By this time we may realize that part of our anger is also toward God. Couldn't he have guided life differently? We can let him know how we feel by expressing our anger toward him. If there is a convenient object available, we may want to give it a kick or throw it to the floor. Is this childish? Perhaps it is the *wisdom* of a child. Better to kick an object that has no feelings—like a toy—than to kick a person or ourselves. After we have thus expressed our anger in the consciousness of God's presence, we will probably feel more at ease—even cleansed.

Some of us are more aware of our depressed feelings than of our anger. Actually, we can help ourselves in our depressed feelings by using this same procedure. This takes more effort when we are this depressed because we lack motivation, and we may also have to deal with denial. Most people don't feel very angry when depressed. But if we persist in confronting the fact that despite feeling futile we are also angry, we will be able to locate an initial focus for our anger. In depression, this initial focus may well be ourselves. In the consciousness of the presence of God, we can tell ourselves off—call ourselves any names that seem appropriate at the moment. Next in line will probably be God, for not preventing us from being such miserable bunglers. After we let him have our anger, others will begin to emerge in our consciousness. They too need to be "told off." I have followed this procedure when depressed feelings were descending on me, and I have felt much less depressed afterward.

COMBINING BACH'S AND ELLIS'S THEORIES

Most of us are probably somewhere in between being openly angry and hiding our anger behind a façade of serenity. It is usually best then to combine the two approaches. Family therapist Theodore Dreikurs advises angry parents to withdraw to the bathroom and ponder the matter when they feel anger rising, rather than impulsively lashing out at their child. In other words, catch it early.

In thus withdrawing "to the bathroom," we can enter into an immediate counseling session with God. First we can let our anger out to him, expressing what we would like to do to certain ornery people. After this catharsis, we can raise questions in God's presence about the assumptions that lay behind our anger. For example, perhaps "the child deliberately defied me, and in our family nobody is allowed to get away with such defiance." Is this stand a matter of parental egotism or of care for the child? The amount of anger may indicate that in the child's defiance the parental ego perceived a direct threat to its self-esteem, and reacted instinctively in the face of the threat.

Now we can evaluate the assumption or belief against the background of our chosen identity. Against the larger perspective of faith and our calling through this faith, is the threat to the parental ego—or pastoral ego—really a threat? The moment we question our reactions, we begin to separate the *behavior* of the child or obstreperous layperson from the *person* of the child or layperson. The behavior angers us, and the child needs to know this, but the behavior is not the child, or the layperson, or the church official. Consequently the child needs to be assured of our love—our agape—when we express disapproval of the behavior.

After this "counseling session" with God, we may decide that we overreacted. Perhaps we read our own memory tapes into the situation and were reacting primarily to them. At any rate the anger is subsiding, and we are glad we didn't say anything to the child (or the layperson or official) because we no longer interpret the incident in the same way. In fact, we might be embarrassed now had we done so. Anger can destroy perspective, and can also arise from distorted assumptions, interpretations, and beliefs.

But the anger may not subside after this counseling session. Then the situation is obviously still a problem, and we need to consider dealing with it directly. Some ways of doing so may only exacerbate the problem; other ways are more likely to resolve it. We are more likely to use the latter ways *after* we have first dealt with our anger in the presence of God.

9. The Biblical Pattern for Healthy Communication

With every impressive Christmas Eve service I attend with my family over the years, I am made more acutely aware that God's entry into the human scene in Jesus' birth radically transforms human life. It gives our personal universe a new center, which in turn influences all aspects of our lives. The sense of meaning and purpose and hope provided by the incarnation forms the basis on which our reason operates.

THE NATURE OF OUR UNIVERSE

In attributing anger to irrational beliefs and assumptions, Ellis assumes that when people are rational they more or less reason in a similar way. Actually, the way our reason operates is highly influenced by assumptions we make about the meaning and purpose of life, and these assumptions are based largely on faith. Consequently we may come to different rational conclusions depending on our differing assumptions about values and priorities. A reason that functions within the perspective of faith in God functions within a universe differently from a reason that functions within the perspective of faith *without* God. Such a faith is belief in something other than God as ultimate meaning and value, whether it be human reason, moral goodness, American culture, the scientific enterprise, the capitalist or socialist economic system, an atheistic worldview or one's own self-sufficiency.

The Christian faith actually enhances Albert Ellis's approach (discussed in the last chapter), because the universe the church provides for the functioning of human reason is much more caring and affectionate than the graceless and yet fallen universe perceived by Ellis. This faith, based on the advent of God into human lives, projects a universe in which the usual threats to human existence are less threatening. "If God is *for* us—and his incarnation says that he is—then who can be against us?" (Rom. 8:31). If the existential threats are diminished by the coming of Christ, then we have less "reason" to be frightened, and consequently less "reason" to be angry in reaction to our fear.

The way we reason is predisposed by how we interpret the human scene, and how we interpret this scene is predisposed by the assumptions of our faith, regardless of what kind of faith it is. The Christian faith in particular, with its vision of a universe with Christ at its center, provides the kind of rational beliefs that reduce the need for anger—particularly for anger as a secondary emotion, which is the only kind of anger that a cognitive therapist such as Ellis recognizes.

SCAPEGOAT OR LAMB?

By the same token, the approach of Bach or Rubin can be viewed as a way of "being angry but not sinning" (Eph. 4:23) In spite of misgivings over anger in our culture, anger in itself is not sin. In fact, because anger in its primary role is a response to injustice and oppression, *not* to be angry in the presence of oppression is more likely to be sin. How can we care about the victims of oppression and not be angry concerning their oppression? Therefore we need to affirm our anger and not deny it, and to do so without sinning.

As previously described, the initial phase of affirming anger is to let it out in the presence of God. The therapy implicit in this catharsis is based on the concept of Christ as the Lamb of God. As differentiated by Episcopal Theologian Fitzsimmons Allison, Christ as the Lamb is not a scapegoat. In early Israel the scapegoat ritual consisted of the populace driving a goat with verbal and physical abuse into the wilderness to die. In contrast the ritual of the sacrifice of the lamb was conducted within the temple by the priests as an offering for reconciliation.

The ritual of the scapegoat was abandoned early in the history of the Old Covenant and has no carryover into the New Covenant. In contrast, the ritual sacrifice of the Lamb in the Old Covenant is carried into the New Covenant in the sacrifice of Christ as the Lamb of God.

Scapegoating as an outlet for anger only increases the anger. The brutality in scapegoating indicates that this need to afflict pain on another, once it is met, only whets the appetite for more cruelty. This pattern holds true whether our scapegoat is the clergy, for our anger toward God, or a member of the family, for our job frustrations; or ourselves, for our anger toward others. Once the process of scapegoating begins, the dynamics are set in motion for accelerating this destructive bent.

In contrast, letting our out anger on Christ as the Lamb is therapeutic. We can be aware of this process even while we are doing it. As Allison points out, letting our anger out on the Lamb makes anger manageable, because his sacrifice keeps us responsible. Scapegoating, however, feeds off and into our self-righteousness. We justify our attacks on scapegoats, usually by making them seem less than human in one way or another. But the Lamb keeps the responsibility where it belongs, namely with us, because we are responsible as fallen human beings for the death of Christ. "Our sickness," says Allison, "is our destructive anger." It culminated in the crucifixion of Christ. "Our medicine is God's taking our anger. If we do not give it to him, we are not healed of it."[1]

Letting our anger out on the Lamb prevents our warm anger from congealing into cold anger. Rubin uses these terms to describe what happens to anger when it stays with us as an unresolved passion. Actually, cold anger is really no longer primarily anger, but has become resentment and hostility and hatred. These are actually destructive attitudes as well as feelings, and unlike our feelings, *are* sinful. As attitudes in which we approach the present moment, resentment, hostility, and hatred distort our interpretation of this moment. In projecting hostility into relationships, we create more anger, which leads to behavior destructive to the realtionship. To prevent such destruction, we need to deal with our anger while it is yet warm.

DEALING DIRECTLY WITH THOSE INVOLVED

After discharging our anger in the presence of God, laying it on the Lamb, we are more capable of being sensitive and respectful with the people concerned. To reenforce this sensitivity, we may need to recondition ourselves. Most of us are conditioned to be insensitive and disrespectful—directly or indirectly—to those who offend us. We can *re*condition ourselves through meditation. Meditation, religiously understood, is a way of responding to God's Word by imagining or visualizing our behavior in accordance with this Word. Meditation, like the catharsis of counseling, is practiced in our consciousness of the presence of God. To recondition, we fashion mental pictures in meditation in which we "see" ourselves responding sensitively and respectfully to people who have angered us. This process helps us differentiate between the person and the behavior, so that we see behind the offensive behavior a frightened, hurt, insecure, or self-rejecting person. Once we see the person in this light, we can feel compassion for him or her. Moved by this compassion, we can visualize this person healed of hurt, and secure in the realization of God's love. These pictures are prayers to God of intercession for the person.

Using meditation in this way conditions us to treat others—even those who anger us—as God has treated us. It is the *person* who is justified by grace, not his or her behavior. The person is loved unconditionally, even while his or her behavior leaves something to be desired. Because we ourselves receive this kind of love from God and his people, we can give it to those who show by their disturbing behavior that they obviously need it.

SHARING HOW WE FEEL

After dealing with our stress in these ways, we ought to be better prepared to work things through with the people concerned. Yet we may decide not to do so. Perhaps, we feel the person in question may not be ready for such an encounter. Or the timing may not seem right, because of other considerations. So we decide we can live with the annoyance for the time being in the hope that "seeing" the person behind the behavior will generate enough compassion to balance our irritation.

Or we may conclude that now *is* the time to deal directly with the concern, either because the person or people in question may well be open to dealing with us if sensitively approached, or because we ourselves need to do so for our own peace of mind. Once we come to this conclusion, it is best to act rather than procrastinate, and to make the needed contact to initiate the process. And once involved in the actual process, it is well to "own" the problem from the beginning. We are dealing with *our* stress and therefore we need to share with the other how we feel, expressing concern about the relationship, the behavior. This approach is a direct application of "speaking the truth in love" (Eph. 4:15). Sharing with another what is going on within us is sharing the truth about ourselves. The compassionate spirit in which it is shared tends to open the other to receive. In contrast, an attacking approach, whether direct or disguised, leads the other instinctively to close up in defensive protection.

An approach that *shares* our disturbed feelings with the other person prepares the way for dialogue. In contrast, an approach that *confronts* the other with his or her faults encourages instead of dialogue, a reactive defensiveness. Although the other's faults as well as our own may come out in the dialogue of shared feelings, the other is more likely to feel supported rather than attacked when this happens. This approach dissipates an incipient power struggle where somebody wins and somebody loses, and provides instead a caring atmosphere where the words *win* and *lose* have no relevance.

Although the purpose in dialoguing directly concerning anger is initially to reduce our own stress, the ultimate purpose is to "gain the brother, the sister" (Matt. 18:15). Many more of our conflicts with others would be resolved, and the stress relieved, if we went directly to the people involved and shared in this manner how we feel. The point is, of course, not to tell them off, or even to tell them they are "wrong," but to share with them our feelings about the problem.

Several years ago I was disturbed by the actions of some colleagues, and consequently felt uncomfortable in their presence. For the sake of the relationship, I decided that I had to talk to each of them personally and inform them of my feelings. It was not easy to make the overture, but I believed I had to do so. Nor were the conversations easy. But the end result— once the initial defensiveness and offensiveness subsided— was a caring dialogue that strengthened our friendships.

Sharing with others—particularly with people whose relationships we value—where we are, and what is going on within us, marks the difference between a private person whom nobody is sure they know and an open person who feels less need to conceal. The private person feels safe in remaining hidden, not having sufficient trust to risk exposure. The needed trust is not simply trust in the one with whom one shares, but trust in God, whose care for us is larger than any particular person's trustworthiness. The development of this trust heals previous wounds so that we are ready to risk additional hurt in seeking the satisfaction of warmth, security, and intimacy that comes only from opening our hearts to other people.

Moreover, we are reluctant to share not just our troublesome feelings, but also our positive feelings. In an address in our community, popular author Father John Powell spoke of his regrets that his father died before either of them ever told the other that he loved him. About two weeks later, a woman approached me in a public place and asked if I was the one who had introduced Father Powell. When I told her I was, she shared with me her experience.

"I took my mother with me to hear Father Powell," she said. "We hadn't been getting along very well for some time, and since we are Catholic I thought his lecture might help. But when he told us to take our parents in our arms and tell them we love them, I said under my breath, 'You don't know my Mom!' It was uncanny. Every time I would raise an objection in my mind to what he was saying, he would answer it. So I decided I was being given a message, and that night I took a deep breath, hugged my mother, and told her I loved her. She stiffened up like poker and didn't say a word. It wasn't very encouraging, but since I had taken the first step I was determined to continue. A couple of days ago I thought I noticed a slight relaxing of her tension when I hugged her. Then last night—so soft I could barely hear her—she whispered, 'And I love you too.' It is changing our whole relationship. Now I'm going to work on my brothers and sisters!"

She had discovered a simple yet largely unused resource for revolutionizing relationships.

GENUINE DIALOGUE

We would considerably reduce the stress in our lives if we were more honest and direct in all our personal contacts. This approach leads us into genuine dialogue, which can take us into expansive dimensions of knowing that otherwise are never explored. During the past seven years, my wife and I have been conducting workships as a ministry for spritual growth because we believe that the workshop format of structured sharing is a very supportive and controlled way of encouraging people to share themselves. The caring that emerges out of such sharing is a strong incentive to develop more open relationships.

There is a risk, however, in such sharing. Not everybody is trustworthy, and not everybody can keep a confidence. So the process may backfire. Therefore we need to count the cost before embarking on what is for some a new experience. The workshop approach is a safe way to initiate or to further encourage personal openness. It can strengthen our confidence so that we can better endure possible rebuffs and disappointments in our quest for more satisfying relationships.

Genuine dialogue is a rather rare experience, because of our defensiveness, subtle or obvious. We usually have our "radar" working so that we can detect threatening innuendoes in our conversations and screen them out. This is why it is hard to get someone to listen to you if you really want to share your hurts. Grieving people, for example, find it frustrating when they need to talk about their feelings of loss. People continually deflect them with familiar clichés or pious reassurances. Some even respond with silence or change the subject. The result is that these grievers can't dialogue in any genuine way even when they want to.

Have you noticed how you can *not hear* what you don't want to hear? One way not to know is not to hear, so that "what you don't *hear* won't hurt you." If you can't miss hearing what you don't want to hear, however, you may take the next precaution, which is to minimize its importance. A child may give the signals that he or she is hurting, for example, and the parents may stifle the cry for help with a reprimand such as "If you would do what I told you to do, these things wouldn't happen!" Or a husband may say to his wife when she expresses dissatisfaction, "I can't see what you're complaining about—other women don't have it half as good!"

Why do people stifle compassion in the face of pain? Because it is unsettling to hear about the pain, and we want life settled. We are afraid of trouble because it threatens our control, and we don't want to hear anything that might indicate trouble. Even in counseling, for example, when we pastors believe we have figured out the other person's problem, it is disconcerting to hear from the counselee—or from others— information that threatens to enlarge the scope of the problem as we had envisioned it, or to throw doubt on our diagnosis.

Because there is a certain security in having things all figured out, we may screen out disturbing information.

Such resistances to hearing what is disturbing, however, only produce more trouble. The idea seems to be that if I resist hearing what is threatening, the trouble will be minimized. But the reverse is true: the more open we are to hear, the more the trouble is eased.

10. Making Decisions That Are Genuinely Our Own

Some of us lose control of our lives because we agree to do all sorts of things we really don't want to do or don't have the energy to do. We fear people's displeasure if we refuse, and are hesitant to damage their image of us. So we say yes when we would like to say no, not because of our convictions, but because we are reluctant to perceive the other's disappointment. But because as finite human beings under God we are limited, we need to accept this reality and make limiting choices. People who try to carry too much may end up dropping everything.

Even a person as wise as Norman Cousins had to learn this lesson the hard way. After he wrote *Anatomy of an Illness*, he was faced with one lecture tour after another, with very little time in between to relax. When he returned home for the Christmas holidays, he very much wanted to cancel his January appointments and stay home. But his associate reminded him that his January tour was already composed of postponed and deferred dates. "You've just got to do it," she said, "You couldn't get out of this thing unless you had a heart attack or something like that."

Said Cousins, "My body, which had been listening to this, furnished the perfect excuse." Three days later he had a severe heart attack, and not only his January engagements but *all* engagements were canceled. Reflecting on this experience, Cousins said, "If there's something you really don't want to do and you want out of it, your body gives you the out."[1]

Seeing beyond ourselves to God can give us the courage we need to do what we couldn't do just looking at ourselves—and then our bodies may not have to provide the way out. We can make our decisions strongly—that is, *consciously*—rather than letting them be made for us by acquiescence or by delay. Then our bodies do not have to substitute for our indecision.

In the pastoral profession, with so much pressure to please and to conform, we pastors can grow in our ability to be our own people and to make our own decisions, and to make them *wisely*. Our commitment, or calling, is the guiding principle for this decision making. This commitment is secured by God's commitment to us. God's calling to us provides the "gestalt"—the context—that helps us interpret the issues. The context is the whole within which the parts fit together to make sense. Because deciding within this context is really a response to God's call, we are able to cope at least to some extent with the fear of making decisions that others may not like. We can live with our decisions when they are consonant with our identity.

The gestalt fashioned by our commitment is also temporal, in that within it past, present, and future all hang together. The stabilizing element is our trust in the higher power, in which we see ourselves as under God. Within this dynamic, we are relieved of the necessity always to make the right decisions, because our self-understanding includes our own limitations and shortcomings.

If you are ambivalent about accepting responsibilities or doing favors, you can be sure that if it continues this double-mindedness will produce stress. If, however, you are honest and direct with people and say yes when you mean yes and no when you mean no, and do so sensitively and kindly, you can control your life in these matters. You can pace yourself and avoid accumulating obligations that can overwhelm you.

Some people may have a conflict over these decisions that you make. Yet if you make avoiding conflict as your priority, you are heading for trouble with yourself. Conflict is not in itself bad. In fact, it can be good, depending on how you manage it. Since conflict is inevitable in the clergy profession, the challenge is to accept it as a positive potential and manage it accordingly. We can take comfort in Jesus's words, "Woe unto you when all men speak well of you" (Luke 6:26), and accept the unresolvableness of some conflicts. We live in a fallen world with fallen people, including ourselves. Our goals regarding harmony not only may be unrealistic but may be projected by our own ego needs.

Any creative work needs limits. Workaholism as a way to prove value, success, or worth, won't work, any more than slacking off in work will prevent us from being judged by our work. The demands and deadlines of the parish ministry inevitably lead to logjams and pressures before which some pastors flee into apathy, and others plunge ahead with determined intensity.

My desk has become a symbol of my state of mind. It measures over six feet in length and is four feet wide—the largest I could find. In spite of its size, I seem not only to fill all the corners but the middle as well—and then I begin to pile vertically. Then my mind feels as disorganized as my desk looks. I can't find things because they are hidden under other things. I waste time and energy looking for them, which only increases my frustration. Finally I realize it is time to clean off the desk. As I do, not only do I find things, but I also begin to feel relaxed. When the desk is completely cleaned off, my mind feels equally as uncluttered. I am back in control.

Deadlines create pressure because we depend on them to motivate us to do work. They are projections of our internalized "parent" looking over the shoulder of our inner "child" to keep us at the job. If we develop an inner-directedness—what champion runner Mary Decker calls "really wanting to do it"—we can finish the work before the deadline exerts its pressure. For example, sermon preparation takes no more time and much less stress to complete a sermon ahead of time than does working up to the last minute.

Since limits are needed in our work, *we ourselves* need to set them. If we let guilt, the need to please, or the fear of not living up to others' expectations make those decisions for us, we will fight them inside. Making our decisions from our own inner-directedness rather than from external pressures does not mean that we won't decide to do what is difficult for us— what frightens us or exposes us to risk. Our own image of ministry and our own sense of identity may predispose us in this direction—to call on a difficult person, for example, rather than waiting for him or her to contact us. Although the task may be difficult, if we have made the decision we will be at peace rather than resisting the decision as though it were imposed from outside. When *we* make the decisions, we can take the consequences with much more grace than when we have let double-mindedness undermine our integrity.

By listening to your own spirit, mind, and body, you can discover your own pace and plan your life accordingly. Emergencies, of course, upset any plan, and they should. But emergencies are really not the problem, rather, it is the habit patterns they initiate. I find it very hard to get back to a balanced pace after I have had to abandon it for emergencies or other pressing obligations. There is no real *logistical* reason why I can't return; rather, I feel a psychological resistance. Perhaps you've noticed this phenomenon. Once we are "revved up," our sheer momentum keeps us going. The other side of this inertia, of course, is that once stopped it is hard to get restarted.

My own resistance to returning to a balanced pace once I've accelerated is also based on my fear of getting behind in my schedule. I've been there! I know what it's like not to be ready to preach on Sunday morning. I know what it's like to get behind on deadlines in graduate theses and other projects, or to feel dismayed after a disappointing class because as the teacher I had not given it enough preparatory thought. These memories are traumatic and because I care for myself I don't want to put myself into such a position again. So the fast pace helps me stay ahead. But because I'm not balanced, the fast pace that keeps me ahead of schedule is also stressful. I keep wondering, am I *sufficiently* ahead?

A sociological analogy to this personal trauma over getting behind in schedule is the trauma many people experienced in the Great Depression. People who experienced financial loss during that period of deprivation rarely recovered from the trauma. They seemed never to be able to feel financially secure, regardless of how well they had recovered from their Depression losses. But how much do you have to have to feel secure once you have been traumatized by insecurity? I was a pastor of a congregation in the good times that followed World War II. Inflation was low and employment was high. But my members were veterans of the Depression and were reluctant to take on any project that involved debt because "it could happen again"! In fact, they were quite sure that it *would* happen again. (And of course it has, to many communities but long after their ominous anticipation.) These people continued to live in fear of being traumatized once again by heavy financial reverses.

Again, our sense of pastoral calling helps us cut through the resistance and reaffirm our commitment to live balanced lives. Although we are creatures of habit and become habituated to a fast pace, we are also creatures of freedom who can decide—consciously and single-mindedly—to stop old habits and start new ones. We *can* take control.

To actualize this freedom, we need to strengthen our commitment, and we can do so by listening to the Spirit. The search for wisdom takes us to many sources. One of these sources, as indicated previously, is listening to our own spirit. We do this best, however, when we also listen to the Spirit of God, whom St. Paul says bears witness with our spirit that we are children of God (Rom. 8:16). Since God speaks to us specifically through his Word, a direct way of listening to the Spirit is to meditate on his Word. Despite all the controversy that has ensued of late from our attempts to define the Bible as the Word of God in a rational way, the functional definition remains unscathed. The Bible is a means of grace—a means through which the Spirit of God speaks to our spirits. If we take the time to let the Bible be this means of grace in our lives, we will receive the "mind of Christ." He is "formed in us" by his Spirit (Gal. 4:16).

Listening to the Spirit is not confined to solitary meditating on God's Word. The means of grace was given to a *fellowship* of believers. The Spirit speaks also through the feedback we can receive from this fellowship. We need to listen to our brothers and sisters in our community of faith, and in other communities as well.

The search for wisdom lies in this complex system of resources. Together with listening to our own voice of experience, we listen also to the voices of others, believing that the Spirit of God speaks to us through all our experiences within the context (the gestalt) of our commitment, which is reenforced by our focus on his Word.

God is not the taskmaster we fear; rather, the taskmaster is our own ego, with its internalized demands to fulfill some image that supposedly establishes our worth. But our life is more than our work, including our ministry, even as grace is more than the fulfillment of any goals. God is bigger than our limits, and therefore we can with grace accept our limits.

11. Remaining Positive in the Midst of the Negative

Dealing religiously with stress is no escape from reality, but rather is a positive way of coping with reality. There is no way in this fallen world to escape frustration, defeat, failure, reversal, sorrow, and all the stress that goes with each. For example, ten years ago we experienced the sudden and tragic death of our oldest daughter. I had ministered to many grieving people, and now grief had come to us. At the memorial service, a colleague grasped my hand and—with a frightening honesty—said, "If it were I, I don't believe I could take it." Strangely enough, his words were comforting. Now I *knew* he understood. We had been hit, and hit hard.

A public letter from our mayor and his wife, who had experienced a similar tragedy, contained these words: "Perhaps the most moving letter we received was from a friend of our daughter who said, 'We all tried to help but nobody could.' " Again, this admission was strangely comforting. They knew he understood. Their letter went on: "We're consoled often by a rabbi's telling us of an old Hassidic saying about death: 'First comes grief, then contemplation, and finally joy again.' We're still in the contemplative stage, with some joyful memories and some terrible ones. Twenty-six years is a long and yet a short time to have a child. She leaves a gaping hole in our lives."

I talked recently with a woman whose husband died suddenly of a heart attack. She was still in a state of shock and kept saying, "How fragile is life." I thought of the words of the Scripture, "What is your life? For you are a mist that appears for a little time and then vanishes" (James 4:14).

Some people become disillusioned with their religion when hit by heartaches. Perhaps they assumed that because they were believers such things would not happen to them. Intellectually they would probably deny this assumption, but their gut reaction may say otherwise. In R. F. Delderfield's novel, *To Serve Them All My Days*, as dramatized on television's Masterpiece Theater, the teacher David's wife and two children were killed in a car accident. The principal of the school, who was also a clergyman, attempted to comfort David as he received the news, but David was inconsolable. Later, talking with his wife, the principal said that David's was the worst situation he had ever witnessed and that he felt he had blundered in his clumsy attempt to console.

"At least you didn't ask him to trust God," she said.

"No, I know he is an agnostic; so I wouldn't do that," he said. "But that is what I'd do if anything happened to you, my dear."

"I know you would," she answered, and then, expressing her own religious disillusion, said, "But your God didn't do too well today."

Similarly, newspaper columnist Russell Baker lost his father by death when he was just a boy. He admired his father and needed him very much. "After this experience," Baker wrote, "I never cried again with any real conviction, nor expected much of anyone's God except indifference, nor loved deeply without fear that it would cost dearly in pain."[1]

A terrible loss to be experienced so young! Considering some of the religious teaching children receive about God, which is really a disguised attempt to protect them from knowing the real world, it probably is no wonder that Baker's trust in God was one casualty of this trauma. At the same time, the loss of trust in God only compounds the loss of the loved one.

Psychiatrist M. Scott Peck, in his book, *The Road Less Traveled*, comes to a conclusion opposite to religious disillusionment. Peck feels the significant point is not that bad things happen to good people but how few times such things happen compared to what one might realistically expect. So imbalanced is the ratio that, Peck believes, a force must be at work in the world protecting us. This force he calls *grace*:

The existence of grace is prima facie evidence not only of the reality of God but also of the reality that God's will is devoted to the growth of the individual human spirit. What once seemed to be a fairy tale turns out to be a reality. We live our lives in the eye of God, and not at the periphery but at the center of His vision, His concern.[2]

Our gut-level hope that as religious people we can escape the traumas of a fallen world is probably reenforced by our awareness of what Peck has noticed, namely, that a friendly force in the universe tips the balance so that bad things are the exception rather than the rule. When the exception hits us—no matter how amazingly small the percentage of such things happening—it now feels like 100 percent.

In fact, we have no assurance in our Christian faith that bad things won't happen to us. We can hope and pray they won't, but there is no breach of contract on God's part if they do. In fact, reading the Bible might even lead us to conclude that because we are Christians we may have *more* trouble: "Through many tribulations we must enter the Kingdom of God" (Acts 14:20). However, this statement does not express a capricious imbalancing on God's part, but a taking into account of the cross, namely, the sufferings that can come from being a follower of Christ in a fallen world.

THE RESOURCES WITH WHICH TO COPE

What we *do* have, as believers, are the resources of faith to cope with bad things should they occur. When things seem to close in on us, when cares and frustrations pile up and we sag under the strain, or threaten to explode or implode, we can take the leap of faith in the direction of God, who is hidden in these troubles. And thus we can find room to live and breathe once again.

The experience is like trying to run with the football during a game, when you are faced by a solid line of the opposing team's defense. There doesn't seem any possibility of getting through. Then you see your own offensive linemen push a hole through that line, and you run through it into the wide-open field beyond. Reality, when we are in the mind set *as God*, is only the opposing line of defense. When our mind set is *under God*, reality is the hole being pushed through that line. We interpret what we see with the mind, the vision, of hope.

This leap into the wide-open space of faith may be what St. Paul meant when he said, "Widen your hearts." In contrast to the mind as intellect, the heart is the seat of our feelings, attitudes, and passions. A wide heart is one that can enter deeply and fully into relationships. Paul said his heart was wide. But he believed the Corinthians' hearts were restricted, hindering the development of the their relationship. "You are not restricted by us," he said, "but you are restricted in your own affections" (2 Cor. 6:11–13).

We are restricted in our affections by distrust, suspicion, resentment, timidity, and our own low self-esteem. Our faith helps us to leap through these restrictions into the wideness—the open field, or open space—of security in the presence of God. There are risks in taking the leap—a hidden tackler could come out of nowhere—but there are greater risks in remaining restricted, trapped behind the scrimmage line. When you feel restricted in your affections, overwhelmed by the futility of an impenetrable line of obstruction, see by faith the space opening before you, and claim it!

In an earlier chapter I referred to a pastor-counselee who thought his problem was unchangeable; I asked this man whether his belief that with God all things are possible had the power to bring about this change. He answered, "The power is there. The real question is whether I can receive it." Although he raised the right question, he unfortunately raised it as a doubt. He was "restricted in his affections," and the first step to receiving would be to "widen his heart." But people who are timid, distrustful, and defensively repressed shrink back from the leap of faith that such widening implies, and prefer instead the safety of confinement.

To trust means to let go of preconceived notions of what is possible and impossible so that we are open to surprise. The grace that Peck sees operating in human life is often received through surprise. It is not only in anticipated ways that God is perceived but in unanticipated ways as well. If his ways are not our ways and his thoughts are not our thoughts (Is. 55:8), we need to leave room beyond our own understanding for the hiddenness of God to become manifest. Grace by its very nature is not accounted for by rational deduction and logical anticipation.

We need to leave room for the God whose thoughts are not necessarily our thoughts in how we interpret the moment, the situation, or the opportunity. Our interpretations, based on our own repertoire of mental imagery, are not only subjective and therefore partial, but also to varying degrees, distorted. Trust means opening our hearts and minds to a perspective beyond our own, precisely because we are aware that our own perspective is too limited to encompass the totality of reality in any given moment or event.

But trust in the God of grace goes with the story of this grace. Historian Martin Marty, in an address given at my seminary, stated that he had been asked by a prominent periodical to write an article on his trust in the American way without going into the religious interpretation of this way. Marty said he declined because whatever trust he had in the American story is based on *The Story*. He meant that his trust in America is not justified by anything in the U.S. society but only by the story of God's grace, which can give meaning to the American story as well as to other stories. The "world out there," said Marty, "doesn't offer much basis for trust." But the story of God's coming into human life in the person of Jesus Christ provides the context within which all phases of human life derive their meaning and thereby their basis for trust.

It can be difficult to hold to this trust in a world where God seems so hidden and our affections are so restricted. Media portrayals of life in this world only reenforce the popular view that God and his story are irrelevant to a realistic assessment of people's real interests and desires. But are these portrayals realistic? Really not. Rather, they present the viewpoint of their designers. The problem is that they purport to be realistic when they are more likely to be propagandistic.

I have always been interestead in motion pictures and have continually attended the movies and watched television dramas. I can't escape the conclusion that, with some exceptions the media present life as a one-sided secularism. The viewer is left with the impression that religion—particularly in the areas of sexuality and morality—is essentially irrelevant to the modern interpretation of human living.

A form of ministry I would suggest for clergy and their laity is to attend selected movies together and afterward discuss the values implicit in the movie and its realism or the lack of it, especially whether religion was recognized as an integral part of life as it is presented in the drama. The group could also brainstorm concerning what they might do as Christians collectively with other groups to bring pressure to bear on the media for a more realistic representation of human life. As someone close to media production said to me, "Reality doesn't sell; only illusions sell." Even so, the illusions presented do not have to be so consistently and selectively devoid of religious interests.

So from where comes the reenforcement for a life view that includes the reality of God's grace? The answer now, as well as in previous ages, is in the support system provided by a community of faith. We need the help of others who function within the perspective of faith even as they need our help. Each of us in the community of faith has his or her own personal story that is based on *The Story*. We need to hear these stories and to share our own for a mutual strengthening of our faith in God's story.

The people of God are the people *for* God. They reenforce each other to provide a balance in a world imbalanced by its own fallenness. These people hold to a positive life perspective even when events might provoke a negative view. They reenforce the transcendent dimension of our being that is so easily submerged by the value system of our culture. In this way we support and encourage each other to carry on!

This community is needed also for the clergy. If you feel limited by the responsibility of being pastor to the people who could provide you with support, you can organize a support group of brother and sister clergy in the community, including, if desired, also their spouses. If someone—you—takes the initiative, the people you contact will probably be interested. Some may drop out after a while, but a nucleus usually continues and new recruits can be added to replace losses. This kind of fellowship—an extended family—supplies the interpersonal support that reduces stress and enhances health.

A FILLED SPACE

The space into which we leap is not simply a space devoid of stress. Nature abhors a vacuum, and God created nature. The space is filled with "the peace of God"—a sense of serenity that "passes all understanding." This peace will "keep [literally, *guard*] your hearts and minds in Christ Jesus" (Phil. 4:7). This fathomless peace protects our inner selves like an armed guard against the invasion of stress.

The fact that the prayer of Alcoholics Anonymous is called the Serenity Prayer, even though it is equally a prayer for courage and wisdom, shows the value placed on serenity by people recovering from the curse of addiction: "God, give me the courage to change the things that can be changed, the serenity to accept the things that cannot, and the wisdom to know the difference." When the courage to act and the wisdom to act wisely are not sufficient resources for the stress of the moment—when there is nothing we can do to change an otherwise intolerable situation—the peace that passes understanding enables us to live as positively as possible within what appears to be a thoroughly negative situation.

This inner serenity rests on the awareness that we are not abandoned to the chances of fate in these threatening situations, even though we may seem to be. Rather, God is still God, and we are in God's hands, although it is only with the eye of faith that we can perceive their protective embrace. Serenity is an inner possession that actually does *guard* us against the destructive effects of hard and destructive times. It is the needed counteractive force to the invading stresses that could stifle any interest or meaning in life. It is a eustress in that we can feel it and it feels good.

The movie called *The Three Brothers* is one of several fine low-budget Italian films that very sensitively depict the significance of common life experiences. The three sons have left their rural home to establish themselves in the city. The occasion for their return is the death of their mother. Their peasant father possesses the serenity that his urbanized sons seem to lack. After seeing the film, I read an account of the director's special tribute to the veteran actor who played the father. After describing what a good influence the actor was on the company the director said, "He is one who is at peace with himself— with life." The actor himself was no longer bedeviled by the anguish of being a human being. What I noticed in the character he played was obviously something this actor possessed within himself.

The fact that he was an older man, of course, may have something to do with his serenity. Aging helps exorcise the demons that can bedevil us when we are younger, demons largely inherent in cultural pressures on us to prove our worth. With aging, one is more likely to come to peace with who one is. But this process is not automatic—one can also become more bedeviled with age, and more than aging is needed to bring it about.

In fact, the very traumas and tragedies that go with life in a fallen world, potentially destructive through they may be, can also be a means by which these demons are exorcised.

Their place is eventually filled by the serenity that is beyond all intellectual comprehension. It would be next to impossible accurately to depict this serenity on the movie screen by the skills of acting alone without becoming maudlin on the one hand or not getting it across on the other. What came through in this film was the good fortune that the actor possessed what the character called for. The director may well have picked him for this reason.

EUSTRESS—GOOD STRESS

Selye's coined word for good stress, *eustress*, has never made it into our vocabulary. This is unfortunate because we need a word for good stress. Otherwise bad stress gets all the attention. The space into which the leap of faith takes us is filled with eustress, even though it was described as peace. The New Testament word for peace, the Greek word *eirene*, from which we get the English word *irenic*, contrasts with our use of *irenic*, which denotes a state more devoid of stress than filled with it. The serenity that fills the open space of faith is the energy of harmony, resonating on the same wavelength with the Spirit. It is a peace characterized by power and strength. The word *enthusiasm* would be a synonym if we stayed with its root meaning, in God, or inspired by God. The peace that passes all understanding is moving, dynamic, energizing, enthusiastic, passionate.

Peace alone cannot fully describe eustress, even as it is not alone as a fruit of the Spirit. Its dynamic character joins peace with joy. Even as peace is depicted as passionate, so also can joy.

In the Bible, the word *passion* is used to denote suffering. The Passion of Christ, for example, is the suffering of Christ. It is also used to denote human desires. Since its use in this latter category is largely with self-centered covetous desires, its connotation is largely negative, being synonymous with *lust*. Yet the anguish involved in suffering, and the energy involved in desiring, reveals the aliveness indicated by *passion*. In fact the word is also used synonymously with the Greek word *energeo*, from which we derive the word *energy*. Both words (*passion* and *energy*) indicate *experience*, involvement. Passion in all its meanings is the opposite of apathy and detachment.

Passion as suffering and passion as joy are not simply two different meanings of the same word. Suffering and joy have much in common, even though they describe experientially opposite states. Suffering in its passion of agony can deepen one's capacity for the passion of joy. My wife and I, and our children, have ourselves experienced this deepening in our own suffering as a family and have observed it in the evolution of others out of their devastating distresses. It is not that joy replaces agony, but rather that it develops alongside of it. Although the agony subsides as the joy grows, it can also return. When it does, it retains its paradoxical affinity with joy.

The New Testament word for joy, the Greek word *chara*, is closely related to the Greek word for grace, *charas*. We lose this connection between *joy* and *grace* in our English translation, but in the language of the early Christians joy comes from grace. In providing us with a security that does not depend on proving ourselves, grace releases our energies for involvement in life for its own sake.

Joy is expressed in a warm outreach and response to life. Through grace we can accept our habitat and be a part of nature, including nature's fallenness. Joy is our response to the uniqueness of each person, a fascination with the image of God still reflected there along with the sinful and the demonic.

Joy is obviously part and parcel of the fruit of love. Love as *agape* is love that can take people as they are and love them warts and all. Such love is therefore a powerful stimulus for creating community, because it transcends a love that depends on chemical attraction or moral acceptance, and is consequently inclusive rather than exclusive. It helps me to think of love as *loving*—a dynamic, reaching, initiating oveture. Since it comes to us through the grace of God, agape allows us to be open to surprise in our value judgments of others. Agape is a eustress, the energizer of community, allowing each person to be different and still be a part of the whole, even as each fruit is different and yet all are one fruit of the Spirit.

Love, joy, and peace mutually stimulate each other. They constitute eustress and the positive energizers into which all the distresses can be converted. Other fruit of the Spirit follow love, joy, and peace but they all depend on these three for their development. "The fruit of the Spirit is love, joy, peace, patience, kindness, goodness, faithfulness, gentleness, self-control" (Gal. 5:22–23).

We know and will continue to know the distress of life. We also know and will continue to know the peace that comes when we are under God. With this peace we will know the good stress of life with its joy in involvement and love for living. This is eustress, descriptive of what in religious language we call "the resurrected life."

12. The Cross and the Resurrection

The paradox of eustress in the midst of stress, of joy along with suffering, of living positively in the midst of negative experiences, is symbolized in Christianity by the paradoxical relationship between the cross of Christ and his resurrection. In an analogous way, our own experiences correspond to these two focal events in the New Testament story. Our downs are comparable to the crucifixion, and our ups are comparable to the resurrection. Yet the relationship is more than a comparison. We are actually identified with Christ in these experiences. Dying and rising is the description of the dynamic of personal or spiritual growth in contrast to the linear or progressive description of growth that is characteristic of the world of nature.

SINNERS AND YET JUSTIFIED

The tension between living in a fallen world and living positively with this fallenness is interrelated with the tension between our being fallen people and living positively with our own fallenness. These tensions are realistic for those who interpret their own stories within the larger context of God's story. God's reconciling love in Christ gives us the courage to accept our fallen situation because this love also provides the hope of victory over our fallenness. In the language of our theology, this tension is described as the paradox or dialectic between (1) being a sinner and (2) being justified in God's sight at the same time (*simul iustis et peccator*). A similar paradox applies to our surroundings. While it is a fallen world in which we live, it is also "My Father's World."

We are not justified before God, or for that matter, before ourselves, by possessing eustress. In fact, it is the other way around. Because we are justified by God's grace—accepted as we are by him and therefore also accepted by ourselves even in our distress—we are likely to experience also eustress. By the same token we are not condemned by God, and therefore not by ourselves either, for having distress. Forgiveness, justification by grace, acceptance as we are, and unconditional love are all ways of describing this Good News that enables us to be positive while still acknowledging and even experiencing the negativities of evil, pain, and tragedy. Good news generates eustress. It is the watershed for continuous new beginnings. The old does pass away; the new can come! (2 Cor. 5:17).

THEOLOGY OF THE CROSS AND THEOLOGY OF VICTORY

The theology of the cross and the theology of victory provide the balance for a realistic understanding of life. They correspond on the experiential level to knowing the passion of pain and knowing the passion of joy. The theology of the cross focuses on the fallenness of the world and on our own personal fallenness. This theology gets its name, of course, from the crucifixion of Christ, when a bad thing happened to a good person. "God spared not his own Son" (Rom. 3:32). According to the theology of the cross, God is hidden in suffering, in the tragic, in the crucifixion, and in our symbolic crucifixions. We see him there by faith and anticipate his victory even when he seems most to have failed, because this theology, although focused on the cross, implies the resurrection.

Although it fits reality, the theology of the cross does not fit the American dream. This dream is one of success, not failure. A good example is the inability to "digest" the outcome of the Vietnam War. Americans are not supposed to lose wars. According to our history books, we always win them; as a bumper sticker says, "Thanks to our Veterans we are Number One!" But by any sober appraisal of Vietnam, however, we lost, even at the height of our investment with 600,000 troops. We lost because with 58,000 U.S. soldiers dead and many more wounded, the end result was precisely what we went to Vietnam to prevent—the total occupation of Vietnam by the Viet Cong. In addition we felt obligated—to our credit—to open our doors to thousands of Vietnamese, Laotians, Cambodians, and Hmong (a mountain people allied with U.S. troops) to save them from retaliation from the victors when we ended our involvement. But how can a failure to achieve an objective be integrated with an ethos that is modeled on success? The frustration continues into a madness stage in our national obsession to be Number One in the nuclear arms race.

The American dream is not confined to national enterprises such as wars. It influences even the seminary where I teach. When I visit our alumnae in pastoral conferences, I hear the complaint that at the seminary we do not prepare our students for failure. We talk about the theology of the cross, but our mind set is fashioned more by the American economic model of continuous growth.

I believe this criticism is valid. We teachers in the theological seminaries tend to romanticize the parish ministry. We picture it in glowing terms, even though all of us have left it for the teaching ministry. Romanticizing the parish ministry has the same deadly effect on the actual experience as does romanticizing any other human enterprise or institution, including marriage. Philosopher-psychologist Sam Keen says that "romance is the jewel in the crown of capitalism. . . . We grow up thinking that some magic day it will happen."[1]

It would be amazing if this same sociocultural and economic romanticism did not slip into our churches and church institutions. And of course, it has. Churches behind the Iron Curtain or under rightist tyrannies are under no such romantic illusions. Nor should *our* churches be under such illusions, even though the fallenness in our midst is more subtly discerned than in the horrendous oppression in the police states.

Yet the theology of the cross is only one side of the paradox.

The other is the theology of victory, which is based upon the resurrection of Christ. At times God comes out of hiding, as it were, and we experience his presence in his Word, in the Sacrament, in our everyday experiences. There are times of victory over evil, of healing disease, of transcending cultural values, of spiritual ecstasy—here and there and now and then. Such victory is "now and then" because the theology of victory also implies the cross. For many people in our culture, the basic want and need from religion is help to bring about change. In their need to halt the nuclear arms race, many young people in the United States and Europe are returning to the churches. Obviously the sporadic stands the churches have taken on this issue have given young people the hope that through the churches something can be done. People experience the same need for change in their personal lives when bad feelings, bad health, and bad relationships—all generators of stress—move them to look to religion for something better. The theology of victory sustains these hopes. Clergy are the symbol of such hope—both to the laity and to each other.

DISTORTION OF THE CROSS

The theology of victory, however, is always in tension with the theology of the cross, and vice versa. The human mind has a difficult time holding on to the "both-and-ness" of a dialectic or paradox. We seem to need the simplicity of "either-or," particularly when we are trying to function *as God*. The "both-and-ness" of constructive tension seems too open-ended for the sense of control that such a mind set needs. Yet when we lose the tension by focusing on *either* the theology of the cross *or* the theology of victory, to the exclusion of the other, each becomes distorted in the process.

Consider the theology of the cross without a dialectical tension with the theology of victory. The loss of the paradox thus leaves the reality of evil without any balancing reality of hope. The result of such one-sided concentration is that we become fixed in defeat. We actually program ourselves to defeat, to failure, to illness, and to all the stress that goes with them—and we consign the world to the same fate. Being religious in this imbalance, we clergy do our negative programming almost as martyrs for the "glory of God."

Yet by this very imbalance we are denying our potential under God for change. We get a perverse sense of comfort out of not recognizing the possibility for change, because if change is possible we may bear some responsibility for effecting this change. Then we feel guilty for not doing it and our stress level goes up. Many people—including us clergy—will do most anything to avoid the misery of guilt. One way to do so, of course, is to believe that nothing can be done that would make any difference. A focus only on the theology of the cross—or on its secular and cynical counterparts—is an example of this avoidance of responsibility. Such a focus relieves us of any complicity in our own failures, defeats, and illnesses and even in the sorry state of society. Our need for a simplistic understanding—an uncomplicated "either-or"—really protects us from our own self-judgement. So long as we see any situation as a complex result of interrelated causes, we ourselves may be one such cause. And if this is so, we cannot escape from our responsibility, and consequently, cannot escape from our need to confess our guilt. Moreover, denying the possibility for change may protect us from guilt, but not from stress. All denial processes produce stress, because none is foolproof and the truth is always threatening to reveal itself.

People who have learned to accept inevitable situations, negative as they may be, have obviously achieved a level of maturity. Yet acceptance should not be equated with inevitability, except, of course, where this is the only reasonable conclusion. If one's leg is amputated, for instance, acceptance of this situation means accepting the inevitability of having only one flesh-and-blood leg. But the pastor I mentioned earlier, who had "accepted" his problem as inevitable, was not overjoyed to hear that something could be done about it, because that possibility laid an obligation on him. Acceptance, in this instance, was not as much an evidence of maturity as an escape from being a responsible person. In addition, the safety that comes from not venturing is bolstered by the lack of a vision of hope. Where they have no vision the people perish, only because they have no incentive then to risk venturing into the new and thereby stifle their own development.

Religion is frequently used to bolster this defense against guilt. Ironically, the Good News for resolving guilt is often distorted into a way of avoiding guilt. We use it to sanctify our fatalism; we say, "I guess that's the way it's supposed to be (or not supposed to be)." Implicit if not explicit in this fatalism is pious resignation to God's will. Obviously, I can bear no responsibility for and therefore no guilt over what is God's will. Although certainly other forces are at work in the world than human freedom, a belief in predestination that leaves no room for a dialogue with freedom is really an escape from the judgment that freedom necessarily entails, and a pseudoantidote to stress.

Yet the denial of freedom does not keep our freedom from functioning; it only represses our conscious awareness that we are exercising it, which in turn usually "predestines" this freedom to a self-destructive use. A good example is our contemporary attitude toward aging, which is largely a negative foreboding of an inevitable, soon-to-catch-up-with-me deterioration of body and mind. Of course, aging is inevitable. Its specific effects, however, vary widely with individuals and cultures. Its effects also bear some relationship to the decisions people make regarding how they live, which can slow or hasten the inevitable process as well as indicate which effects one is more likely to experience. For example, as noted earlier, women who do not exercise regularly as they age and whose diets are lacking in calcium are more likely to develop osteoporosis, the brittle bone disease that afflicts more elderly women than men. Yet if people choose to believe that they are sure to develop such degenerative diseases, then they feel protected from any judgment on themselves for hastening or even developing them. Such fatalistic attitudes negatively express our own determinative potential. We program ourselves to experience what we consider inevitable.

Another form of this predestination syndrome is the attitude toward ourselves that says, "That's the way I am—that's me!" I was counseling with a couple that was having marital problems; the wife would invariably take this position when confronted with her destructive behavior. I almost got the impression she was proud of her behavior, although it was obviously an obstacle in her marriage. At one time in her development, this behavior had served as a survival measure, and served her well. But now the issue was no longer survival; rather, it was marital harmony. Yet she still persisted in her dated reaction—which had become an equally dated preventative of stress. And "If this is the way I am—that's me," then how can I conceivably believe I could or should change?

Genuine self-acceptance in one's own situation, however, is open to alternatives. If change is possible, one accepts the responsibility that this alternative entails; and if change is not possible, one can also live with this alternative. In fact, such genuine acceptance may remove whatever psychological obstacles to change that may be present.

For example, the Bowdens were married for seven years and had no children, although they deeply desired them. Then Mrs. Bowden attended the birth of her sister's baby. It was a particularly difficult birth, and Mrs. Bowden was extremely shaken by the experience. She confided to a friend that she was now willing to accept her childlessness so that she would never have to go through anything like her sister's experience. Yet three months later, to her amazement, Mrs. Bowden discovered that she was pregnant. After adjusting to the shock, she discovered she was very happy about being pregnant.

If our mental positioning is under God, we leave room for the mind of God. Things do not have to be "either-or," black or white, for our protection. The seeming contradiction inherent in paradox only points to the possibilities that lie beyond simplistic and defensive human logic. Although lowering our defenses initially heightens stress, it eventually leads to a lifestyle that lowers stress.

DISTORTION OF THE RESURRECTION

By the same token, the theology of victory by itself, apart from a dialectical tension with the theology of the cross, also becomes distorted. Such a focus ceases to reflect the reality of fallenness and becomes fixed in illusion, programming its adherents to deny the full intensity of evil and tragedy, particularly in their own involvements. Our tendency to read "foreverness" into our present perception of reality is an aspect of the illusionary potential of the theology of victory. Although our feelings are not identical with our perspective, they greatly influence it. When we are up in spirits, for example, we assume at our visceral level that we will never go down; and when we are down, it seems just as impossible that we will ever be up. The psalmist knew about this propensity from experience. "When I felt secure, I said, 'I shall never be disturbed. You, Lord, with your favor made me strong as the mountains. Then you hid your face, and I was filled with fear' " (Ps. 30:7–8). Also when we are in good health, we have a hard time seeing that we may ever get sick. We may even critically judge "sickly" people. But when we are ill, we wonder whether we will ever be well again—and we envy those who are healthy.

Taking the theology of victory by itself, with no theological reference to the *down* side of life further distorts the tendency to predict "foreverness" by fostering our denial of the negative. When we are programmed to be up and believe we will never go down, we become wholly unprepared for a relapse. The potential for denial can manifest itself to an amazing degree, even in the face of an obvious relapse, although to maintain itself it usually needs a heavy dose of chemical or religious tranquilizers. Stress is not eliminated by denying the negative aspects of life. Like the evil we refuse to recognize, we are simply less aware of such stress. But stress is even more destructive then because we do not recognize its earlier warning signals. It is more likely then to enter into our consciousness through the symptoms of physical illness.

But reality can become so negative that even a theologically fortified denial system can no longer maintain itself. Then it is not uncommon for the person to flip to the opposite distortion in the theology of the cross. Some people have been uncritical followers of a religious leader, for example; and when this leader's "clay feet" can no longer be denied, such followers may become cynical about any religious leader or about religion itself. The same is true of political leadership. For most of his life, for example, an uncle of mine believed the Republican Party was the only party to which a Christian could belong. But toward the end of his life, he became very cynical about all politicians. "They're all a bunch of crooks," he would grumble. Callous acceptance of injustice and corruption predisposes one to see what one expects to see.

These two extremes in denial were both manifested in the sex-with-pages scandal in the U.S. Congress. One loyal follower of a censored U.S. Congressman blamed the high school girl for seducing him. A spokesperson from his own office defended him by saying that if all sexual transgressors in the U.S. Congress were expelled, there would be no Congress left. And uniting both these extremes is their common purpose of denying any personal responsibility in the Congressman himself.

Like its theological opposite, a distorted theology of victory protects us from facing our own complicity in evil, and therefore is an escape from confession, as well as from the stress that precipitates confession. Such a distortion leads to a theology of glory, or triumphalism, which maintains its positive note by minimizing the reality of the negative. Theological triumphalism has gone hand in hand with American optimism, one aspect of which is belief in continuous progress or growth, whether economic growth or church growth. Yet those who adhere to this theological distortion have within themselves the "dreaded opposite" of cynical pessimism, even as those who follow a distorted theology of the cross have within themselves the dreaded opposite of a secret hope in which they dare not trust. Stress, though subliminal, is present. So it is not unusual for people to swing from one extreme to another during their lifetime.

Rather than swinging to either extreme, we can learn to live in a tension between the two. Such a perspective then is both realistic and positive. Hope is implicit in the theology of the cross—God will triumph over what seems to be his defeat. The resurrection is the background against which we look at the cross. And evil is implicit in the theology of victory. Not only is the cross the background against which we look at the resurrection, but that cross itself is a judgment on us all. Northrup Frye, prominent teacher of the Bible as literature, says, "Jesus is the one figure in history whom no organized society could possibly put up with. The society that rejected him represented all societies—the whole of humankind down to ourselves and doubtless far beyond."[2] As part of "the whole humanity," each of us is guilty of complicity in the crucifixion of Christ. The late Bishop James Pike said it was necessary for us to see ourselves as agents of Christ's death to be the recipients of his forgiveness.[3] We have the same anger as those who were the historical perpetrators of his death, and our anger, like theirs, is healed by his passion.

THE WAY OF CHANGE

The theology of the cross and the theology of victory need to remain in constructive tension. By combining realism with positive anticipation, this tension opens the door to the Spirit's guidance. There is the crucified life; there is the resurrected life. The cross and the resurrection do not diminish each other, any more than do the passion of suffering and the passion of joy.

There are scarcely any limits to the tragic and the demonic in life: Jesus was crucified. I receive Amnesty International's newsletter, *Matchbox*, in which are reported story after story of documented torture and death inflicted on the prisoners of conscience within the rising number of police states. Many miniholocausts continue to take place. As I am writing this book, the Christian and Druse (Moslem) militiamen in the mountains of Lebanon are kidnapping, torturing, and killing each other—all in the name of God! And there are also holocausts of omission. To save their own skins—usually jobs or promotional potential—people remain quiet or turn the other way when someone is being treated unjustly. We have seen this happen in church institutions.

We know also our own fallenness. We can be shocked at what can enter into our own minds or come out through our own lips when we are motivated by self-centered defensiveness or self-aggrandizement. We show all too ominously our affinity with other sinners.

So also there are scarcely any limits to love, to self-giving, to joy, to the resurgence of spirit, to peace, or to mercy: Jesus is risen. For example, Father Maxmillian Kolbe of Poland volunteered to replace another inmate of a Nazi concentration camp who was scheduled for execution, because he had no family, while the other man did. The Nazis accepted his offer. In 1983, Pope John Paul II canonized Father Kolbe—for his sacrifice—during a ceremony at which the man for whom he gave his life was present.

Just a week ago as I write, three people were thrown into the shark-infested waters off the coast of Australia when their boat sank. One of them, his leg severed by a shark, deliberately swam away from his companions to draw the sharks toward his own blood so that they might possibly be saved. And one of them *was* saved.

We ourselves may be aware at times of the intensity of our own caring for others, and even amazed by our spontaneous overtures of concern and compassion.

The same paradox that exists in the relationship between the theology of the cross and the theology of victory exists also in our own being. We live in the sphere of time and are subject to its limits; yet we transcend time in our relationship with God, who is eternal.

We are in the world and yet not of it (John 17:11–14). We are a part of our culture but are also called to other values and priorities. We are in the body, a part of nature, bound by nature's laws; yet in another sense we are free from its limits through an imaginative mind that can take us anywhere.

We participate in the life of sensory perception with its limits and in the world of science. We also participate in the life of the Spirit, in which we see with the eye of faith what science cannot give us.

Living in the awareness of this paradox in our being and in the world in which we live will give us the mind-set for eustress instead of distress. Because in this mind-set we are realistic about ourselves and our world, we waste less psychic energy in defending ourselves against these realities. When we trust in the One who, though crucified is resurrected, his vision of hope will buoy us through times of external stress.

Epilogue: Religion Works with Science to Heal

Business columnist Lynda McDonnell calls job stress "the tuberculosis of our day." It is a killer, and we haven't yet achieved a cure. Her comments were in reference to the newly established Minnesota Stress Council. The Council's purpose, as described by its organizer, John Lennes, resembles an attempt "to grab a handful of smoke." There's no question that job stress can damage workers' health and productivity; McDonnell quotes Joseph Rosse (professor at the University of Minnesota Industrial Relations Center) who pessimistically concludes that help in this regard will not be forthcoming from science: "Scientific researchers have found little, if anything, to work conclusively," so that "scientific advice could be a long time coming."[1]

This conclusion is important for clergy for the following reasons. First, clergy's own job stress is understandable in the light of the job stress in general. Second, those in the congregation with jobs obviously need help with job stress. Third, this stress is not a problem for science alone to resolve, but also one for the clergy's own expertise—religion. If the thesis of this book is correct—that a biblical psychology or anthropology is a necessary base for understanding the nature of stress—then science needs religion to develop "advice." On the basis of what has been repesented, we need a more holistic approach to the problem than science alone is capable of providing.

A HOLISTIC APPROACH

A holistic approach would certainly include science, but it would also need to include a religious approach to the human being as created in the image of God. Science and religion, therefore, provide the needed combination to deal effectively with stress. It is unfortunate that these two were ever put into competitive or antagonistic positions, because they need each other for a holistic approach to human betterment.

Science can investigate the reality of religion but cannot explore its essence. It can only ascertain its effects on people. This contribution, however, is not to be minimized. Science has been valuable to religion in precisely this way. Religion, it has been said, brings out the best and worst in people. Motivated by religion, people have demonstrated great generosity and self-giving. Religion has also motivated people to commit the most diabolical and heinous acts of cruelty. There is bad religion and good religion. Science can help in distinguishing between these. Pastoral theologian Don Browning, for example, used the scientific principles of psychotherapy as a standard in evaluating four theories of the Atonement of Christ. On this basis, he determined the theory that was the most beneficial for health and healing, namely, the victory theory (Christus victor) that pictures Christ as victorious over the enemies of sin, death and the devil.[2]

Disciplines such as the psychology of religion (which is really the psychology of religious experience), and the sociology of religion (which investigates the corporate dimensions of religous practices), and anthropological studies of religion in various cultures, are all needed but limited fields of investigation. The investigators are scientists—basically, outside observers. But objectivity, so necessary for scientific pursuit, can go only so far in the study of religion. To explore religion from the inside, the explorer must go beyond the role of scientist and take on the experiential role of a participant. Subjectivity rather

than objectivity is needed to *complete* the process of understanding. This is why Søren Kierkegaard said, "Subjectivity is
truth." Only when objective truth becomes known subjectively
does it become truth for the subject—for me.

In contrasting objective science with subjective religion, we
should not conclude that subjectivity is the only way to knowledge. Objectivity and subjectivity do not oppose each other;
rather, they complement each other. Subjectivity by itself can
lead to illusion. We need the objectivity of science to balance
our subjective conclusions in order to evaluate them. For the
same reason, we need the objectivity of other people to test
out our own subjective insights. Precisely because it is so
subjective, religion needs its corporate dimension. The objective Bible and the objective Sacraments, for example, were
given to an objective body, the Church, within whose rites
and fellowship individual subjectivity is both stimulated and
monitored.

Given this holistic approach to knowledge, religious resources are needed for coping with stress. The matters of
values and priorities and the questions of meaning and purpose that play so vital a role in the generation of stress are
matters and questions of *ultimate* significance. They are essentially religious in nature, or at least philosophical, and they
are not the domain of scientific research.

Yet religious people suffer stress. Ministers of religion have
it. Philosophers have it. As we have seen, the office of the
ministry or the priesthood is no different from other professions in our culture so far as susceptibility to the pressures of
competition and comparative standards for evaluation are concerned. Being *in* the world, clergy have as much difficulty as
laypeople do in not being *of* it, and they tend to measure their
satisfaction with their job by the familiar ego satisfactions that
are part and parcel with job satisfaction elsewhere. The grass
on the other side of the fence gets that same greener hue that
it does for teachers, farmers, accountants, and homemakers.
Clergy—like philosphers, like scientists, like the rest of us—

have what the New Testament calls the *flesh*, an inner tendency to be self-centered, envious, and possessive, to the detriment of their own and others' well-being.

When religious people—clergy or laypeople—experience stress, they are showing that all of us, Christians, atheists, Moslems, and Jews, are one common human family. They may also be showing that they have trouble applying their religion—like the rest of humanity. Religious teaching and religious resources often remain abstract, it seems, when and where we most need to apply them. Our spottiness in applying at the present moment and to the present situation our own religious beliefs is our common lot, but one that I believe we can do something about. And we need the help of science to do so, for science can clarify not only the effect on us when we use religious resources but also the mechanics of becoming open to using these resources. Science can help the rubber to hit the road in the application of our faith.

Pastoral theology (the branch of theology I teach) is by definition a combination of religious teachings with psychological and sociological data concerning human dynamics. This book is an example of pastoral theology. Pursuing this same combination, but stating it from the other side, the Minnesota Job Stress council is looking into the treatment for alcoholism and other addictions as possibly "shedding some light on how best to deal with job stress." The focus in this treatment of addiction is largely the Twelve Steps of the Alcoholics Anonymous Program, a well-known example of a holistic approach to one kind of stress, in which the principles of sociology are combined with a biblical understanding of human nature and a belief in God's grace. It is interesting that people have taken fifty years to gradually see how to apply these steps to many other forms of stress than chemical addiction. It is even more interesting that though these steps were developed from Christian theology, they were developed outside of the organized church.

Religion can become too abstract. Some have tried to prevent this development by pointing out religious parallels to scientific findings—a procedure often attempted with the clinical data of psychotherapy, for example. Yet what is needed is neither abstaction nor parallelism, but integration. Religion provides a theological base from which the findings of science can be religiously interpreted. The early Church Father Irenaeus taught that while the fall into sin disrupted the creative process, God's redemption from the fall through Christ restored it. It is this restoration to which the clergy are devoted in their ministry. The specific focus of pastoral theology is to unite the "Word of God" that is implicit in creation, including the data of science, with the "Word of God" that is explicit in redemption.

I hope this book will provide the wider picture into which these specific applications of pastoral theology fit as parts of a whole.

Notes

Chapter 1

1. Martin Marty, "Reverend Stress," *Christian Century* (15-22 July, 1981): p. 75.
2. Hans Selye, *Stress Without Distress* (Philadelphia: Lippincott, 1974), p. 61.
3. Peter Berger, "Letter on the Parish Ministry," *Christian Century* (20 April 1964): p. 550.
4. "Baptists for Tobacco," *Christian Century* (15-22 August, 1984): p. 768.
5. Selye, *Stress Without Distress*, p. 99.
6. John Parrino, *From Panic to Power* (New York: Wiley, 1979), p. 43.
7. Ogden Tanner, *Stress* (New York: Time-Life Books, 1976), p. 7.

Chapter 2

1. Ogden Tanner, *Stress* (New York: Time-Life Books, 1976), p. 28.
2. Hans Selye, *Stress Without Distress* (Philadelphia: Lippincott, 1974), p. 14.
3. Claudia Wallis, "Stress: Can We Cope?" *Time* (6 June 1983): p. 48.
4. "Heart Attack Risk Rises for Women Smokers," *Journal of the American Medical Association* (December 1983): p. 3A.
5. Hans Selye, *The Stress of Life*, rev. ed. (New York: McGraw-Hill, 1976), p. 209.
6. Donald R. Morse, *Stress for Success* (New York: Van Nostrand Reinhold, 1979), pp. 41, 93.
7. O. Carl Simonton, Stephanie Mathews-Simonton, and James Creigton, *Getting Well Again* (Los Angeles: Tarcher, 1978), pp. 221-25.
8. Wallis, "Stress", p. 48.
9. Tanner, *Stress*, p. 10.
10. Wallis, "Stress", p. 50.
11. Tanner, *Stress*, p. 60.
12. Selye, *Stress Without Distress*, p. 78.
13. Norman Cousins, *Anatomy of an Illness* (New York: Norton, 1979), pp. 35–40.
14. Tanner, *Stress*, pp. 64–65.

Chapter 3

1. Margaret Crepeau, "A Comparison of the Behavioral Patterns and Meanings of Weeping Among Adult Men and Women Across Three Health Conditions" (Ph.D. diss. abstract, University of Pittsburgh, 1980).

2. Nancy Kasselbaum, quoted by Eleanor Clift, "A Matter of Style," *Northwest Orient* 14 (April 1983): p. 22.
3. Maggie Scarf, *Unfinished Business: Pressure Points in the Lives of Women* (New York: Doubleday, 1980).
4. Søren Kierkegaard, *The Concept of Dread* (Princeton, N.J.: Princeton Univ. Press, 1944).
5. Hans Selye, *Stress Without Distress* (Philadelphia: Lippincott, 1974), pp. 122–31.
6. William Sloane Coffin, *The Courage to Love* (San Francisco: Harper & Row, 1982), p. 11.

Chapter 5

1. Søren Kierkegaard, trans. Walter Lowrie, *Fear and Trembling and the Sickness unto Death* (Princeton, N.J.: Princeton Univ. Press, 1954), p. 230.
2. *St. Athanasius on the Incarnation* tr. and ed. by A Religious of C.S.M.V. (London: A.R. Mowbray & Co., Ltd., 1944), p. 93.
3. John Cheever, "Goodbye My Brother," *The Stories of John Cheever* (New York: Knopf, 1978), p. 21.
4. Cheever, "The Common Days," *The Stories of John Cheever*, p. 26.
5. William Sloane Coffin, *Once to Every Man* (New York: Atheneum, 1977), pp. 287–88.
6. Coffin, p. 290.
7. Albert Einstein, quoted in L. Robert Keck, *The Spirit of Synergy* (Nashville: Abingdon, 1978), p. 77.

Chapter 6

1. Søren Kierkegaard, *Sickness unto Death* (Princeton, N.J.: Princeton Univ. Press, 1954), p. 173.
2. Henri Nouwen, *Reaching Out* (New York: Doubleday, 1975), p. 29.
3. Kierkegaard, *Sickness*, p. 172.
4. Robert Schuller, "Blessings Always Boomerang," pamphlet, from Hour of Power, Garden Grove, CA (1978): p. 5.
6. Hans Selye, *The Stress of Life*, rev. ed. (New York: McGraw-Hill, 1976), p. 214.

Chapter 7

1. Salvador Minuchin, *Families and Family Therapy* (Cambridge, Mass.: Harvard University Press, 1974), p. 252.
2. Ogden Tanner, *Stress* (New York: Time-Life Books, 1976), p. 147.
3. B. Carr, et. al., "Physical Conditioning Facilitates the Exercise-Induced Secretion of Beta-Endorphin and Beta-Lipotropin in Women," *New England Journal of Medicine* 305 (3 September 1981): p. 560.
4. Phyllis McGinley, "Reflections at Dawn," *The Love Letters of Phyllis McGinley* (New York: Viking, 1955), pp. 81–82.

Chapter 8

1. Arthur M. Schlesinger, Jr., *The Age of Jackson* (New York: New American Library, 1949), p. 32.
2. Hans Selye, *The Stress of Life*, rev. ed. (New York: McGraw-Hill, 1976), p. 221.
3. Virginia Satir, *Peoplemaking* (Palo Alto, Calif.: Science & Behavior Books, 1972), p. 66.

Chapter 9

1. C. Fitzsimmons Allison, *Guilt, Anger, and God* (New York: Seabury Press, 1972), p. 88.

Chapter 10

1. Beth Ann Krier, "Cousins Says 'Heal Thyself'," *Minneapolis Star* (27 May 1981): p. 1B.

Chapter 11

1. Russell Baker as quoted by Donald Morrison in "Country Boy" *Time* (1 November 1982): pp. 80–81.
2. M. Scott Peck, *The Road Less Traveled* (New York: Simon & Schuster, 1978), p. 312.

Chapter 12

1. Sam Keen, *The Passionate Life* (San Francisco: Harper & Row, 1983), p. 7.
2. Northrup Frye, "The Great Code," *New Yorker* (31 May 1982): p. 104.
3. C. Fitzsimmons Allison, *Guilt, Anger, and God* (New York: Seabury Press, 1972), p. 87.

Epilogue

1. Joseph Rosse, quoted by Lynda McDonnell, "Business/Twin Cities," *St. Paul Dispatch* (18 July 1983): p. B3.
2. Don Browning, *Atonement and Psychotherapy* (Philadelphia: Westminster Press, 1970).

2. Don Browning, *Atonement and Psychotherapy* (Philadelphia: Westminster Press, 1970).

List of Related Books

Allison, C. Fitzsimmons. *Guilt, Anger, and God*. New York: Seabury Press, 1972.

Bach, George. *Creative Aggression*. New York: Avon, 1975.

Beck, Aaron. *Cognitive Therapy and the Emotional Disorders*. New York: International Universities Press, 1977.

Brother Lawrence (Nicholas Herman). *The Practice of the Presence of God*. New York: Image, 1977.

Cousins, Norman. *Anatomy of an Illness*. New York: Norton, 1979.

Ellis, Albert. *How to Live With and Without Anger*. New York: Reader's Digest Press, 1977.

Hulme, William E. *How to Start Counseling*. Nashville: Abingdon, 1956.

Morris, Donald R., and M. Lawrence Furst. *Stress for Success*. New York: Van Nostrand Reinhold, 1979.

Nouwen, Henri. *Reaching Out*. New York: Doubleday, 1975.

Parrino, John. *From Panic to Power*. New York: Wiley, 1979.

Pelletier, Kenneth R. *Mental and Physical Illness*. New York: Ziff-Davis, 1977.

Rassieur, Charles. *Stress Management for Ministers*. Philadelphia: Westminster, 1982.

Rubin, Theodore. *The Angry Book*. New York: Macmillan, 1969.

Satir, Virginia. *Peoplemaking*. Palo Alto, Calif.: Science & Behavior Books, 1972.

Sehnert, Keith W. *Stress/Unstress*. Minneapolis: Augsburg, 1981.

Selye, Hans. *The Stress of Life*. Rev. ed. New York: McGraw-Hill, 1976. Originally published 1956.

Selye, Hans. *Stress Without Distress*. Philadelphia: Lippincott, 1974.

Tanner, Ogden, and the editors of Time-Life Books. *Stress*. New York: Time-Life Books, 1976.

List of Related Books

Allison, C. Fitzsimmons. *Guilt, Anger, and God*. New York: Seabury Press, 1972.

Bach, George and Herb Goldberg. *Creative Aggression*. New York: Avon, 1975.

Beck, Aaron. *Cognitive Therapy and the Emotional Disorders*. New York: International Universities Press, 1977.

Brother Lawrence (Nicholas Herman). *The Practice of the Presence of God*. New York: Image, 1977.

Cousins, Norman. *Anatomy of an Illness*. New York: Norton, 1979.

Ellis, Albert. *How to Live With and Without Anger*. New York: Reader's Digest Press, 1977.

Hulme, William E. *How to Start Counseling*. Nashville: Abingdon, 1956.

Morris, Donald R., and M. Lawrence Furst. *Stress for Success*. New York: Van Nostrand Reinhold, 1979.

Nouwen, Henri. *Reaching Out*. New York: Doubleday, 1975.

Parrino, John. *From Panic to Power*. New York: Wiley, 1979.

Pelletier, Kenneth R. *Mental and Physical Illness*. New York: Ziff-Davis, 1977.

Rassieur, Charles. *Stress Management for Ministers*. Philadelphia: Westminster, 1982.

Rubin, Theodore. *The Angry Book*. New York: Macmillan, 1969.

Satir, Virginia. *Peoplemaking*. Palo Alto, Calif.: Science & Behavior Books, 1972.

Sehnert, Keith W. *Stress/Unstress*. Minneapolis: Augsburg, 1981.

Selye, Hans. *The Stress of Life*. Rev. ed. New York: McGraw-Hill, 1976. Originally published 1956.

Selye, Hans. *Stress Without Distress*. Philadelphia: Lippincott, 1974.

Tanner, Ogden, and the editors of Time-Life Books. *Stress*. New York: Time-Life Books, 1976.

Index